**colour in your**
# home&
# garden

# colour in your
# home & garden

SALLY WALTON & RICHARD ROSENFELD

## An essential sourcebook of decorative schemes

southwater

This edition is published by Southwater

Distributed in the UK by The Manning Partnership
251–253 London Road East, Batheaston, Bath BA1 7RL
tel. 01225 852 727; fax 01225 852 852

Published in the USA by Anness Publishing Inc.
27 West 20th Street, Suite 504, New York NY 10011
fax 212 807 6813

Distributed in Canada by General Publishing
895 Don Mills Road, 400–402 Park Centre, Toronto,
Ontario M3C 1W3
tel. 416 445 3333; fax 416 445 5991

Distributed in Australia by Sandstone Publishing
Unit 1, 360 Norton Street, Leichhardt, NSW 2040
tel. 02 9560 7888; fax 02 9560 7488

Southwater is an imprint of Anness Publishing Limited
Hermes House, 88–89 Blackfriars Road, London SE1 8HA
tel. 020 7401 2077; fax 020 7633 9499

© Anness Publishing Limited 2001

**Publisher** Joanna Lorenz
**Managing Editor** Judith Simons
**Project Editor** Claire Folkard
**Editorial Reader** Joy Wotton
**Production Controller** Ann Childers
**Designer** Mark Latter
**Photographers** Peter Anderson, Jonathan Buckley,
Rodney Forte, John Freeman, Michelle Garrett, Tim Imrie,
Andrea Jones, Simon McBride, Marie O'Hara, Lizzie Orme,
Steven Pam, Debbie Patterson, Spike Powell,
Graham Rae, Lucinda Simmons, Adrian Taylor,
Jo Whitworth, Peter Williams, Polly Wreford
**Contributors** Pattie Barron, Deena Beverley,
Kathy Brown, Lisa Brown, Victoria Brown, Diana Civil,
Sacha Cohen, Stephanie Donaldson, Marion Elliot,
Tessa Evelegh, Mary Fellows, Emma Hardy, Paul Jackson,
Alison Jenkins, Mary Maguire, Maggie Philo, Tabby Riley,
Andrea Spencer, Stewart Walton, Josephine Whitfield

Previously published as two separate volumes, *The
Colourful Home* and *The Colourful Garden*.

10 9 8 7 6 5 4 3 2 1

# contents

# introduction

This book will help you discover the power of colour and understand how it can be used to create the environment you want. The chapters in both the Home and Garden sections are devoted to particular colours, exploring their impact at full intensity and in a range of shades, tints and tones. The colours are shown in real rooms and gardens with many different styles illuminated by both natural and artificial light.

Colour can be warm or cool; it can be calming or excite us. Indoors, colour can make small rooms look more spacious or cavernous rooms feel cosy. It can hide a multitude of sins or bring interesting architectural details into focus. It has the potential to elevate and invigorate your interior decorating. Outdoors, the natural colour of plants can be used to brighten dark borders or soften hard features and to create atmosphere. Often combinations that do not work well indoors can make a real impact in the garden. Be brave and experiment until you find the plants that, in the words of Monet, "make the leap and crackle and blend".

Trust your feelings, explore the possibilities and enrich your life with a greater under-standing of colour.

# Understanding colour

The study of colour in a purely scientific way began with Sir Isaac Newton in 1676. His experiments with light led him to shine pure white light through a glass prism and reflect it on to a neutral-coloured surface. The result was a continuous band of merging colour, ranging from red through orange, yellow, green, blue and violet. The rainbow is nature's version of Newton's experiment. Light passing through drops of rain projects the spectrum colours across the sky.

## The Colour Wheel

To explain colour, scientists constructed the colour wheel, which separated the spectrum into twelve different colours. This was done by first drawing a triangle divided into three equal sections for the primary colours – red, yellow and blue. These are called primary because they cannot be mixed from a combination of any other colours. They, along with black and white, form the basis of all other colours.

The primary colours are placed in an equilateral triangle with yellow at the top, red lower right and blue lower left. A compass is used to draw the wheel around it and then divide it into twelve equal sections. The primary colours then fill the sections opposite their position in the triangle.

Secondary colours – orange, green and violet – are made by mixing equal parts of two of the primaries: yellow and red make orange, yellow and blue make green, blue and red make violet. These colours fill the spaces midway between each of the two primaries.

Tertiary colours are made by mixing a secondary colour with an equal amount of the colour next to it on the wheel: yellow and orange make golden-yellow, red and orange make burnt orange, yellow and green make lime green, blue and green make turquoise, blue and violet make indigo, red and violet make crimson. Arranging colours in this way helps us to see the effects that can be achieved when they are used alongside and opposite each other.

## Colour Theory

It is worth taking time to understand something of colour theory because our perception of colour is mainly a physiological phenomenon. Our eyes encounter different colours as wavelengths of light, and our brains recognize

Using a colour wheel helps us to understand the theory of colour, allowing us to use colour effectively in the home.

ABOVE The rich red tones of these pelargonium petals cast a warm glow on the wall behind.

OPPOSITE These contrasting lamps in shades of red and yellow provide a warm light and are guaranteed to brighten up your room.

and interpret this information. Red, as the colour of danger, is not a random choice: it is transmitted on the highest frequency and is recognized faster than any of the other colours. As a warning, it is immediate. Red advances, appearing closer, while blue recedes. A room in which the walls are painted red will appear smaller than one with walls that are painted blue.

The existence of colour depends entirely upon light. This can be demonstrated by placing a red vase on a table in a room directly lit by a standard tungsten bulb. Turn off the light and the vase is no longer red, but black like everything else in the dark room. The colour of any object is only a visual experience and not an actual fact!

This has all to do with the power of a surface to absorb or reflect light particles. Red appears to be red because it absorbs all the other colours of the spectrum and reflects only the red. Illuminate it with a green light and it will no longer be red but black. It may just be a trick of the light, but that, in essence, is what colour is.

You may wonder how important this is to interior decorating or planting up a border, and the answer is probably not very, but colour is a powerful tool and the more you know, the more chance you have of using its properties to the maximum and benefiting from it.

A hue is one of the pure colours of the spectrum, such as red or yellow, and it can be used to describe other colours. For example lavender has a violet hue, olive has a green hue, or pink has a red hue.

Colours opposite each other on the colour wheel are called complementary. These are colours of equal intensity. When they are combined in equal proportions they make a neutral grey. Alongside each other they are at their most intense. If you concentrate your eyes on a single colour for a few seconds then shut them or stare at a white or neutral grey, you will

find the complementary of the colour you were looking at appears before you. This is known as after image. The eye produces this contrast to achieve a state of equilibrium, returning once more to what is most comfortable and balanced. Artists who study colour theory will sometimes exploit this effect to create discomfort and to arouse emotion in the viewer. When planning a colour scheme it

helps to know the relative power of the different colour combinations, if only so you know which ones to avoid.

Colour contrasts occur on several levels. The simplest to understand is a contrast of hue, which describes the difference between undiluted colours seen alongside each other. Yellow/red/blue, being the primaries, represent the most extreme example of this. There are also hot/cold contrasts – the red, yellow, orange side being hot, and the blue, green, violet side being cold. The most extreme hot/cold contrasts that exist are red-orange and blue-green.

A scientific experiment was conducted involving the same group of people spending time at the same level of activity in the same workroom, which was first painted in cold colours and then in warm colours. The actual room temperature was very gradually lowered and the level at which they first felt cold was 11°C/52°F degrees in the red-orange room and 15°C/59°F degrees in the blue-green room. It was concluded that colour has the power to increase or decrease the circulation. So it really does make sense to paint a chilly room in warm colours.

Another type of colour contrast is light and dark. This contrast is very clear if you look at both a colour and a black-and-white version of the same photograph. Red and green have the same tonal quality and show up as an equal grey on the black-and-white version. Yellow and violet are the most extreme examples of light/dark contrast apart from black and white, which are not colours but tones.

OPPOSITE The varying shades of blue in this table setting complement each other perfectly.

ABOVE RIGHT These grape hyacinths (*Muscari latifolium*) create a sea of blue when they flower in spring.

RIGHT A strong primary colour scheme of red and yellow tulips underplanted with brilliant blue forget-me-nots.

The addition of white to a colour produces a tint, which we call a pastel colour; black darkens a colour to produce a tone.

A harmony is a combination of colours that allows the eye to travel smoothly between them. Colours that are close to each other on the colour wheel will harmonize: orange, yellow and red, for example. Colours that do not naturally harmonize, such as orange and crimson, can be made to do so by the addition of white. Most home decorating paints are highly diluted with white, because the pure colours are generally too intense when covering a large expanse of wall.

## Personal Taste

Quite apart from the science of colour, there is a subjective element to colour choice. People do favour certain colours, and no amount of theory will persuade someone to surround themselves with a vivid shade of yellow or red if they are of a calmer blue-grey disposition.

Fortunately we are all individuals and personal taste varies enormously, but it is still essential to recognize that these basic colour laws exist and to have a good understanding of how colour works. At least then, when you break those rules in a surge of creativity, you will be aware of what it is you are doing.

OPPOSITE **Dashing red dahlias and rich lilac-blue asters illustrate the most extreme hot/cold colour contrast.**

RIGHT **Using slightly softer shades of red and blue, the same contrasting effect can be seen in an interior.**

# the colourful home

Whether you want to brighten a dull corner or completely transform a whole room, this section of the book will show you how. From inspiring features on luscious reds to soothing blues, you're guaranteed to find a scheme that's right for you.

# using colour in the home

It's impossible to be indifferent to colour, since it surrounds you all the time. Its influence on mood is obvious: just imagine walking between concrete walls, sitting in the shade of a leafy tree, gazing into a clear blue sky, or putting on a bright red sweater, and you can immediately appreciate the power of colour. So choosing colours to decorate your own home can seem a daunting task; no wonder everyone spends hours thumbing through interiors magazines and peering at paint charts and fabric swatches, searching for that elusive perfect shade.

Whatever colours you choose, you (and your family) should love them: there's no point in following time-honoured decorating rules to the letter if you end up with a scheme you can't bear – you'll be seeing a lot of it. And you certainly shouldn't pick the shades that fashion decrees if the result will be a room you can't feel comfortable in. Fashions move fast, but rather than following them slavishly you can make the relentless procession of new trends work for you: there's always a new range of colours or patterns from which you can choose elements, to help you create a style that's all your own.

When you decorate your home, you are aiming to provide an environment that is comfortable for you and welcoming for your family and friends. Like the clothes you wear, your home is a visual expression of your character and personality; it should provide a setting rather than overwhelming you.

## Colour and Light

Colour can't exist without light, so the quality and quantity of light in a room is the first thing to consider when decorating. If your windows face north, the light will be cold even on sunny days. If there are trees outside the windows, the room may be paradoxically lighter in winter and spring than it is in summer, when the leafy canopy will cast a green shadow over the interior. In bright light, brilliant white walls may be dazzling and tiring on the eyes, but in any room with good natural light – especially if it has windows facing more than one direction – white decor will take on a fascinating range of tints and shades during the day and into the evening. With a few sharper accents of colour,

RIGHT **A green curtain with a bright red lining provides a striking contrast.**

ABOVE The soft fabric of this orange lamp gives a subtly coloured glow.

A small, dark room can be made to seem larger and brighter by painting the walls in a pale colour. Or, rather than fighting against the limitations of the space, you could try using bright or deep colours to create a cosy, womb-like atmosphere. A white ceiling will open up the room, and a pale floor will give a more spacious feel. At the other end of the scale, very large rooms can be difficult to decorate, too. Against a generally neutral scheme, the judicious use of a single colour in furniture and accessories can help to unify the space.

If you're painting a room, don't forget that colour will be reflected between the walls, intensifying its effect. One blue wall in a hall, for instance, may look perfect; two blue walls might produce an icy cold effect. If, when you've finished, the result isn't what you hoped, it's better to swallow hard, buy some more paint and start again. On the other hand, if the colour just seems too intense, remember that you're not going to live in an empty room – bringing pictures, mirrors, furniture and fabrics into the room will tone down all that strong, undiluted colour.

supplied by accessories such as flowers and pictures, you can bring out the best of these subtle variations.

Don't just think about daylight. You may use your sitting room or dining room mainly in the evenings, so colours will need to work best in artificial light. Deep, rich colours can look dramatic in these situations, but will absorb lots of light. You can also play around with the colour of the light itself, diffusing it through coloured shades or reflecting it from coloured ceilings or walls.

## Creating Mood with Colour

You can exploit the emotional power of colour to create an ambience that suits the function of every room. Colour therapists maintain that a balance of colours throughout your home is important to minimize stress.

Beginning at the front door, a hallway in a strong, warm colour, such as coral, peach or gold, will make your guests feel welcome as they step inside. Warm yellow is a positive colour. In the kitchen, yellow will help you to feel energetic and efficient, while blue will tend to slow you down. Red walls have a warming, enfolding effect, ideal for a dining room; it's also a stimulating colour and will get everyone talking. It's less appropriate in a bedroom, where it might cause sleeplessness. Instead, soft blues can be used to create a relaxing, secure atmosphere. Blue is a familiar, comforting colour — it's the one chosen by most people as their favourite. It's also good for a bathroom, where you could add turquoise and green for their calming, purifying effects.

## Co-ordinating Colours

The following pages will give you plenty of new ideas for colour combinations, and should inspire you to look afresh at your existing furniture, flooring and fabric colours. Consider your home as a whole so that the colours harmonize and make visual sense between one room and the next. In the end, however, decorating rules are made to be broken: originality and surprise make for an exciting environment. Using and understanding colour is an ongoing process: trust your instincts and enjoy experimenting.

ABOVE RIGHT Create a striking colour contrast with this pink and blue cushion.

RIGHT The crisp texture of this cerise lamp makes a bold statement against the blue background.

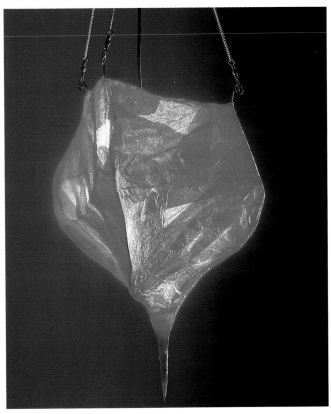

# yellow

The colour of the sun carries within it the power to compensate for a lack of natural sunlight, which makes it indispensable if you are decorating in a dull, grey climate.

Yellow expands, warms and brightens north-facing rooms. Walls that have been painted yellow give off a glow of light, like an aura, which advances to influence the atmosphere of the whole room. Tonally, yellow is the lightest colour in the spectrum, and it is associated with positive moods. Warm, mellow yellows come from natural earth pigments and harmonize well with reds, browns and oranges, whereas the sharp, cool yellows, such as lemon and chrome yellow, are derived from chemicals and look best alongside other cool colours, such as light blue, pale grey and lavender.

"naturally bright buttercups and daffodils
to the metallic brightness of brass and gold"

# yellow palette

The expression "yellow palette" is used to describe those colours in which yellow is the dominant hue. They range from naturally bright buttercups and daffodils to the metallic brightness of brass and gold, and from the palest Jersey cream to vibrant and sharp lemon curd. Those yellows from the red side of the colour wheel will harmonize in all their tints and tones, as will those on the green side. Balance a predominantly yellow colour scheme by adding small touches of its complementaries, blue or purple, and your eyes will rest easy.

BELOW **A background of primrose yellow gives a strong, modern look.**

BELOW **Lemon zest and lime green create an intense citric harmony.**

BELOW **Sunshine yellow roses are punctuated with green foliage.**

ABOVE The gold in these gilded bay leaves has a cool sheen.

ABOVE Orange sorbet brings a warm welcome to a cold steel chair.

ABOVE Tangerine dream gives a sophisticated look.

BELOW Cinnamon spice adds a subtle warmth to walls.

BELOW Cappuccino coffee gives a naturally elegant finish.

BELOW Cocoa brown provides a meltingly rich backdrop.

**This is a refreshing colour**, and its name instantly evokes images of clumps of pale primroses growing on grassy banks in early spring. The colour is like the flower after which it is named: cool and self-illuminating, but with the ability to gather strength and thrive when bathed in warm light.

Primrose appears on the blue-green side of yellow on the colour wheel. Although naturally cool, it carries a promise of warmth, which can be best brought out if it is used in combination with its complementary, a reddish-purple.

# primrose yellow

Nature does not make mistakes with its colour associations, and primrose yellow, pale and tinged with green, provides the relaxing element in a woodland stroll when it is combined with light moss green and deep violet. Use it with white, pale grey and black for a sharper urban look – this is the perfect colour scheme for an airy loft conversion.

ABOVE Yellow flowers add another dimension to this colour scheme. The effect is intense but harmonious, because all these colours have a yellow hue.

LEFT The red chilli (chile) flowerheads perfectly complement the primrose yellow and inject an up-to-the-minute note of heat in an elegantly stylish setting.

# string bottles

Colour alters according to the texture of the surface. These three bottles have been wrapped in string, which matches the colour of the smooth paintwork around them, but their texture makes them stand out. Choose bottles with interesting shapes, and turn them into works of art.

## You Will Need

Ball of string

Glue gun

3 nicely shaped bottles

Scissors

1   Coil one end of the string round like a drinks mat. Heat the glue gun, then apply glue in spokes over the base. Press the string on to them. To make the base secure, draw a ring of glue around the edge.

2   Circle the bottle with the string, working your way up and applying glue as you go. Make sure you get a good bonding on the bends. When you reach the top of the bottle, cut the end of the string and apply glue to prevent fraying. Repeat these steps with the other bottles.

RIGHT Black, white and lemon, combined with the unfussy, straight lines of the stained glass, add an art deco feel. The brave choice of bright lemon for the walls was inspired by the small segments of the colour in the door panels. It works, and the overall effect is stunning.

OPPOSITE The lemon yellow wall lights up the natural light browns of the cane, wood and string in this arrangement.

BELOW AND BELOW RIGHT A clean colour for the kitchen, lemon yellow can be warmed with liberal sprinklings of dark red. Restrict the incidence of other colours and allow the yellow to dominate.

# energizing
colours full of
# lemon zest

# lemon zest

**Lemon yellow is such a distinctive colour**
and so inseparably linked to the fruit that the sight of it can bring the sharp, tangy taste to the mouth. The coolest of the yellows, it has brilliance but no warmth, which gives it a sophistication that the sunnier golden-yellows lack.

The colour was impossible to mix from an earth pigment and was introduced to the artist's and decorator's palette in the late 18th century when chrome yellow, a lead-based pigment, was first manufactured. It immediately became the height of fashion for elegant interiors during the late Georgian and Regency periods. The sombre Victorians did not like it much, but it was used widely in the 1920s before coming back to the forefront of fashion in the 1950s.

# Yellow Jewel Chair

**You Will Need**

Armchair

Medium-grade
sandpaper

Clear wax or silicone

Polish

Rubber fabric

Scissors

Staple gun

Rubber adhesive

Paintbrush

Hammer

Upholstery tacks

Thick artist's card

Transform an old armchair into a desirable object with simple upholstery. Stretchy fabrics make it easier to achieve a professional finish, but any upholstery fabric is suitable.

1 Remove all old covers from the armchair. Sand the varnish from the frame. Seal with a clear wax or silicone polish. Use the old covers as a template and cut the fabric to size, with a generous allowance for the back rest.

3 Cut the fabric to fit the back surface of the back rest and apply rubber adhesive to the fabric and chair. When tacky, apply the fabric, covering the staples and the turned-over edges. Hammer a tack into each corner.

2 Stretch the fabric over the back rest until it is hand-tight and staple it in place. Secure, in order, the top, bottom and sides with one or two staples in the centre, before applying lines of staples to keep the fabric taut.

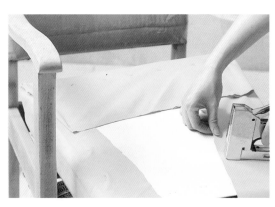

4 Trace the cushion shape on to the card. Cut out and staple to the cushion. Wrap the fabric around the cushion and staple to the card. Attach a layer of fabric to the underside of the cushion using rubber adhesive.

# sunshine yellow

**Golden sunshine yellow exudes ripeness**, warmth and happiness. Its intensity and brilliance can, literally, light up a room that has limited natural light. It can also be overpowering unless the eye is allowed some respite in the form of its complementary colour. Small splashes of cobalt blue and some white will balance the effect without dulling the yellow. When it is used in combination with its true complementary, purple, the contrast is quite visually disturbing.

Imagine a field of sunflowers against an azure sky and you will be seeing sunshine yellow at its best. Seen up close, the sunflower offers us another good guide to which colours combine successfully with sunshine yellow. Natural earth colours tinged with red, such as terracotta, red ochre and burnt sienna, will harmonize well, while deep brown or black will give the most dramatic light–dark contrast.

ABOVE The sunflowers, with their large, brown seed–heads, dominate this group of yellow flowers. Unassuming containers make certain that the flowers are the centre of attention.

OPPOSITE The terracotta wall colour provides a strong, yet harmonious, background for the vibrant sunshine–yellow chair. The flowers enhance the effect by carrying the yellow over into the arrangement and keeping the other blooms within the yellow palette.

# frieze frames

**You Will Need**
Lining paper
Ruler
Craft knife
Yellow emulsion
(latex) paint
PVA glue
Medium paintbrushes
Small, sharp scissors
Green paper
Yellow ochre
acrylic paint

Print-rooms were all the rage in the late 18th and early 19th centuries. Black-and-white prints of Greek and Roman temples and classical views were cut out and pasted directly on to walls in formal framed arrangements, and this pale yellow was the standard background colour. This project shows how to create an elegant print-room frieze with a touch of colour.

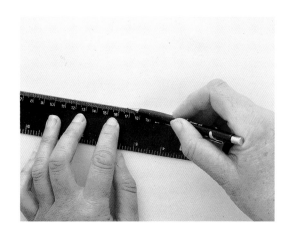

1 Measure the lining paper to the required length and depth of your frieze. Cut along the edge using a ruler and craft knife. Mix three parts yellow emulsion paint with one part PVA. Add a little water to allow the mixture to flow more easily. Use this to paint the lining paper.

2 Choose some motifs and take as many photocopies as necessary to cover the length of the border. Cut them out with scissors. Cut the green paper into equal short lengths. Tear along the top edge to represent greenery.

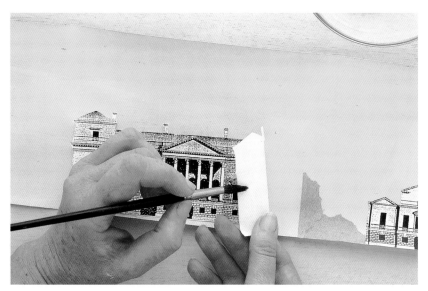

3 Arrange and glue down the buildings and torn paper along the length of the frieze.

Glue down the swag motifs along the top edge of the frieze.

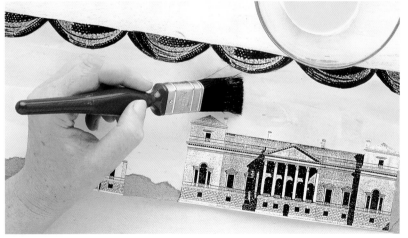

Mix a little yellow ochre acrylic paint into some PVA glue. Then dilute four parts tinted glue with one part water. Brush the tinted, diluted glue over the frieze to seal and protect it.

# shell frames

### You Will Need

Wooden frame
Gold spray paint
Shells
Scrap paper
Strong glue
China marker

Gold highlights a good shape and exaggerates a bad one. The perfect symmetry of these scallop shells is naturally decorative and too fine a gift to be left behind on the beach. Take a few home in your pocket and use them to make this stylishly simple golden frame.

1 In a well-ventilated area, cover your work surface with scrap paper and spray the wooden frame with the gold paint. Let dry.

2 Place the shells on some scrap paper, ensuring they are welll spaced. Spray them evenly with the gold paint. Let dry.

3 Arrange and glue the shells to the frame with strong glue. Mark their positions first with a china marker as each shell is different.

# gold

**Gold, the yellow metal**, has been a symbol of wealth since the beginning of civilization, and because its supply is limited, it has always been highly valued. Until recently gold would not have been used to decorate a home unless it was a palace or a bordello. These days all that glitters is definitely not gold, and you can buy very convincing water-based gold paint in a range of shades suitable for walls and furniture.

TOP Fill gilded seashells with wax to make gleaming candles.

ABOVE Gold can add lustre to special occasions.

LEFT This lovely bentwood chair has been gilded with an application of gold leaf on a white background to give a pale gold effect.

# orange sorbet

**This orange has a light**, juicy quality, which is diluted in intensity but not dulled by the addition of white. It is the colour of orange ice lollies (popsicles), goldfish, red lentils, ripe nectarines and sun-bleached life jackets. It carries warmth that does not overpower in the way that a brighter or deeper shade of orange would. It is a good choice of wall colour for a child's north-facing playroom, especially if the natural sunlight is weak and indirect. It is also good for kitchens and dining rooms, but it is not relaxing and is best avoided in bedrooms or sitting rooms. Accents of cool blue-grey or sage green are complementary, and a metallic silver grey will give it an up-to-the-moment look.

shades of **orange sorbet** burst with irresistible warmth

LEFT The muted orange works particularly well with its complementary colour, blue.

ABOVE Sheer curtains give an impression of warmth.

OPPOSITE Natural wood and silver work well with these orange napkins.

# tangerine dream

**Tangerine is a sassy**, youthful colour, a flamboyant younger cousin to orange. It is full of life and can be used to inject freshness and sparkle. Balance it with flashes of ice blue or pale jade green, but create paths of light cream or off-white between them.

This is a great colour to use in a small bathroom with white fixtures. It looks good alongside chrome, aluminium and bare wood. Use it on a single wall in a contemporary home surrounded by pale, neutral shades, or in an entrance hall, where its welcoming energy will be put to good use. An orange environment is also said to improve social behaviour and make people feel less hostile.

ABOVE Take your inspiration from nature's perfection with Chinese lantern pods to reinforce an orange theme.

OPPOSITE Tangerine looks vibrant alongside its next-door neighbours on the spectrum, red and yellow. White adds light, and a dark pewter grey gives a dramatic contrast.

# shades of orange

**Orange is one of nature's indicators**, showing us that fruit is ripe, that summer has ended and that autumn has arrived. When the sun is low in the sky its light is more gentle than in summer and we can see the true beauty of the colour. Take this idea into the home, using subtle washes of light rather than a bright central light pendant for an orange room.

Team it with natural materials such as raffia, hessian (burlap) and wood to give a minimalist room real warmth. Alternatively, sharpen the orange with silver, as with the starbursts below, to give a wall an expensive-looking wallpaper treatment on a budget. A harmonious mood can be created by using fruit and flowers to carry the same colour forwards into the room.

# cinnamon spice

**The spice's powdery texture and distinctive smell** are inseparable from the colour itself. Try conjuring up a picture of cinnamon swirled through golden-yellow pastry: it is warm, comforting and utterly delicious.

The colour works well when it is applied as a wash rather than as flat colour, and it is best used within the context of its natural associations and origins. This is the colour of baked mud walls, clay pots, worn, polished wood and tanned suede. To show off its richness use it with bitter chocolate and pale cream, accented with small splashes of golden-yellow.

THIS PAGE Natural fabrics in warm cinnamon colours are woven loosely together to create this rustic blind.

OPPOSITE TOP LEFT Brilliant primary colours work well against rusty spice walls.

OPPOSITE TOP RIGHT A pale yellow ochre and cinnamon wash combined with bands of pale green creates the Tuscan villa look.

OPPOSITE BELOW LEFT Natural materials are used in a calm, stylish work space.

OPPOSITE BELOW RIGHT The spice brown colours of oiled and polished wood are rich and varied.

warm, **comforting** and utterly **delicious**

# cappuccino brown

**The mixture of coffee and cream** creates a unique shade of brown with a smart urban edge. Browns like this, together with cream shag-pile carpets and supple suede upholstery, have enjoyed a recent fashion revival. Simplicity is the key to success. Keep the walls white, use dark-stained natural wood for shelves and glass, leather and chrome for furniture, and hang plain blinds at the windows. Cushions and throws in sensuous fabrics – silk, and chenille, for example – can be used to add softening touches, but do limit your choice to shades of brown.

# soothing tones of mocha, toffee and walnut

OPPOSITE **Coffee-coloured walls look good in a modern setting, but good lighting is essential because the colour radiates very little light of its own.**

LEFT **Natural wood floor slats in shades of cappuccino are inset** with broad blocks of pale cream to create a dramatic floor pattern.

BELOW **A simple hopsack cloth set with white porcelain reveals how a limited palette can give striking results.**

# sensuous shades of
## the richest **chocolate**
# brown

LEFT A chocolate ponyskin pattern can be easily stencilled on to a lampshade to give it a Wild West look.

BELOW The real thing – a chocolate and cream sundae.

OPPOSITE An intricately carved wooden screen; the patterned fabric and clay pots re-create a North African look.

# cocoa brown

**Whether you prefer** melt-in-the-mouth milk chocolate or the snappy bitterness of dark chocolate, few of us need to be reminded of its colour. This is the richest of the browns, veering toward red and black in its dark tones and pale mushroom brown when it is diluted with white.

Although it is seldom used as a wall colour, it comes into its own when it is used sparingly with white or a pale earth colour. At its darkest, it can be comfortably surrounded by almost any colour in any degree of brilliance; when it is lighter it is best used with earthy shades. Chocolate brown and ivory white is a popular combination in American colonial-style interiors.

# red

The most prominent of all colours, red demands and receives our attention. One of the three primary colours, whose complementary is green, it ranges through hot orange-red to cool red-violet. Red has both positive and negative associations. In some cultures it is the colour of love and life, in others it represents danger. Decorating with red is considered brave, bold and challenging. In the past red was derived from crushed beetles, baked-earth pigments, and roots and minerals. These days we can choose any shade of red and have it copied synthetically, so we are free to re-create the colour of Georgian dining rooms, Gothic stained glass, 1950s polka dots or faded Tuscan frescoes.

"decorating with red is brave,
bold and challenging"

# red palette

When the earthy rust colours produce warm, friendly and relaxed feelings, the red palette is rich and welcoming, but at the other extreme, where we find purple, steeped in ceremony and magic, it is inclined to make us feel uneasy and anxious. Mix white with any red to dissipate these sensory challenges and create a pastel pink or lavender.

Solid red can be too dominating if it is used over large areas, but it will provide uplift when used as part of a pattern or in splashes as drapes, throws, cushions or floral arrangements.

BELOW **Poppy red is a dramatic colour choice.**

BELOW **Crimson and mauve make a lively combination.**

BELOW **Rusty red is a deep, rich, warm colour.**

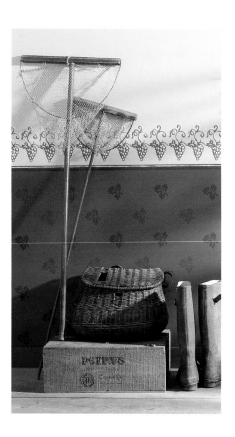

ABOVE Raspberry pink against white walls creates maximum impact.

ABOVE Shocking pink gives walls a modern feel.

ABOVE Pastel pink carries positive connotations.

BELOW Strawberry cream is rich, ripe and simply delicious.

BELOW Vivid violet is deep, rich and cool.

BELOW Purple passion can be tamed with a vibrant aqua blue.

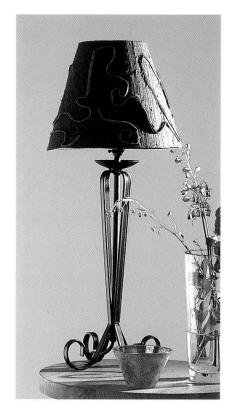

# poppy red

**Anyone who has seen a yellow cornfield** streaked with bright red poppies on a sunny day will know what an unbeatable combination red, straw yellow and sky blue make. Poppy red is associated with bravery and bravado in decorating: you have to feel courageous to choose this colour for your walls, so be prepared to defend your choice! Because red advances visually, it will make a room look smaller if it is used on all four walls, but the effect can be used to advantage in a long, thin room to pull the opposite walls towards each other.

Poppy red works best alongside its neighbours on the yellow side of the colour wheel, because they take their share of its impact. However, it sets up an intense energy field when it is used alongside crimson and violet. For a metallic contrast choose a rich antique gold.

The combination of the bright golden-yellow lampshade and poppy red wall glows like a roaring fire.

cornfields **streaked** with **bright** red poppies

# poppy flowers

Poppies are all the more precious because the flowers do not last long when they have been cut. Luckily, the texture of the petals resembles paper and the simple shapes are easily copied to make very convincing fakes. Use the brightest red paper for the petals.

**You Will Need**

Garden wire

Cotton wool (surgical cotton)

Yellow, black, red and green crêpe paper

Sticky tape

Scissors

Glue

1 To make the stem, cut a length of garden wire. Bend the top to make a loop and trap a small amount of cotton wool in the loop. Cover this in a cut-out circle of yellow crêpe paper. Secure by wrapping tape around it.

2 Cut out three small circles of black crêpe paper, fringe the outer edges and then poke the other end of the wire through the centres and slide up to the yellow bud. Cut out five petal shapes in red crêpe paper and stretch the outer edges until they frill. Glue the petals, one by one, around the centre of the base.

3 Finally, cover the stem in green crêpe paper by winding a long strip diagonally around and securing it at the base with sticky tape.

# crimson skies

**The colour crimson is a red** tinged with blue. It originated as cochineal, a dye made from the dried bodies of insects, which were gathered from cacti in Mexico. Its brilliance and rarity made it a very expensive colour, and its use implied great wealth.

In countries such as India and Mexico, crimson is used in potent combinations with ultramarine blue, banana yellow, lime green and dazzling white. In the softer light of more temperate climates, it imparts a wonderful warmth and sexiness when it is combined with silvery sage green or shades of violet.

# crimson, rust and golden-yellow

OPPOSITE Although the furniture is of Eastern origin, it is ultimately the colour that transports us into an exotic dreamworld. The use of semi-sheer fabric for the drapes means that only the minimum of hand-stitching is needed.

LEFT The brilliant combination of crimson, rust and golden-yellow glows with intensity. This shows us how a sense of mood and place can be established simply through the use of colour.

BELOW Candlelight is enhanced when set off against the colour crimson, as is evident in this rosy winter arrangement.

# pleated tissue blind

## You Will Need

Wallpaper paste
Pasting brush
Hand-made tissue
paper
Tape measure
Scissors
Double-sided tape
Ruler
Pencil
Eyelet tool and eyelets
2 small tassels
Thin, coloured cord to
match tassels
Staple gun
Wooden batten to fit
window recess
2 screw eyes

Delicate hand-made tissue paper makes a surprisingly sturdy blind. To give extra depth to the colour, we pasted two sheets of the crimson paper together. When the light shines through, it vibrates with colour.

1 Mix up the wallpaper paste following the manufacturer's instructions and paste together two sheets of tissue paper. Leave to dry. Measure the window recess, adding 5cm/2in to the width and 15cm/6in to the length. Cut to size and apply the double-sided tape to the sides.

3 On the back of the blind, mark horizontal lines with a ruler and pencil 5cm/2in apart. Fold the blind into regular pleats along the marked lines. Use an eyelet tool to pierce holes on both seams, at the centre of each pleat. Insert the eyelets.

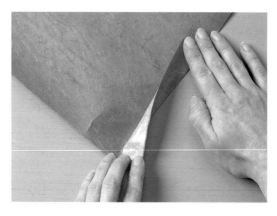

2 Remove the backing paper and fold a 2.5cm/1in hem down each side. Apply double-sided tape to the lower edge of the blind then fold a 2.5cm/1in hem along its length.

4 Tie a tassel to the end of a length of cord and pass it through the eyelets. Repeat on the other side. With the staple gun attach the blind to the top of the wooden batten and place the screw eyes at each end. Thread through the cord so that the two ends hang to one side of the blind.

# rusty red

**Whether it is called terracotta**, red ochre, Indian red, rust, brick red, ox blood or barn red, this colour has a universal appeal, and we all recognize its familiar warmth. The variety of shades, from bright rust through to deep red-brown, can be safely mixed together, and because it is the colour of earth, wood and leather, there are few colours with which it cannot be happily combined. Deep purple, sea green and dark grey are popular choices, and they will look sensational with a pale neutral between them.

Rusty red looks sharp and smart when it is combined with black and cream, but, for a dreamy effect, try pale ice blue, and greens and reds will produce a more rustic result. Use it matt and chalky as a colour wash on walls to give an ethnic look, or as a flat oil colour on skirtings (baseboards) and floorboards.

ABOVE LEFT These two shades of rust red create a rich backdrop for a display of dried roses.

LEFT Elaborate mirror mouldings and elegant soft furnishings contrast with the roughest of paint treatments to create a deliberate look of "faded splendour".

OPPOSITE The lampshade is made from sheets of undyed bark. As the light shines through, the effect is stunning.

# napkin rings

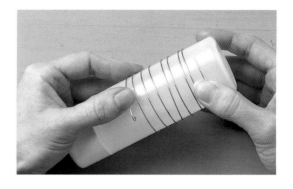

Fine galvanized wire
Ruler or tape measure
Wire cutters
Round-nosed
jewellery pliers
Plastic bottle to use
as former
Glass rocaille beads in
pink and red
Fine silver wire

This is a brilliant project for a rainy day and will bring instant sunshine to the dinner table. The tiny glass beads in shades of pink and red catch and reflect the light, contrasting perfectly with crisp, white napkins. Wired rocaille beads, woven into simple designs, shimmer in the candlelight and make delicate yet sumptuous ornaments for the dinner table.

1 Take about 2m/2yd of galvanized wire and bend a small loop in one end. Wind the wire about ten times around the plastic bottle.

2 Thread enough pink glass beads on to the wire to fit around the bottle once, then change to red and thread another round of beads. Repeat until the wire is full, then bend a loop with pliers.

3 Bend the beaded wire around the bottle to restore its shape. Secure a length of fine silver wire to the first row, then bind it around the others. Do this at two or three other points around the napkin ring. When the ring is complete, wind the ends of the silver wires back around the previous rows to neaten, and snip off the excess.

# raspberry ripple

**A youthful and exuberant red**

that manages to be both energetic and cool, raspberry red's complementary colour is pistachio green, and they are an unbeatable summer-invoking combination. Until recently, only the brave dared use raspberry red as a solid wall colour, but it often appeared in floral patterns. The rosebud wallpapers and fabrics popular in the 1950s have come right back into fashion, but now we have both the paint colours and the courage to match them. On its own, raspberry red can have a cold, rather impersonal feel, but it is very responsive to other colours. For a brilliant Rajasthani-style colour scheme try raspberry red with burnt orange, turquoise, silver frames, lamps and accessories.

ABOVE RIGHT Rich raspberry red flowers are complemented by a soft, white wrapping and a purple bow.

RIGHT To make this bedroom wall colour, a raspberry colour wash has been applied on top of a base coat of yellow. The result is a patchy, glowing pink, which sits happily alongside the orange-yellow woodwork.

**energetic** shades of
**raspberry** red

# shocking pink

**The name says it all**: a pink so arrestingly bright that it stops you in your tracks. It is an extrovert colour, always attention seeking, and even when white is added it manages to grab the limelight. To re-create a 1950s style, use shocking pink with black or white in polka dots or stripes, and, for a 1960s or 1970s look, go for colour clashes by introducing bright orange, purple or scarlet. If retro is not your style, use the pink alongside rich ethnic-looking textiles with other strong, solid colours, such as emerald green or royal blue.

THIS PAGE Shocking pink gives this room a strong contemporary feel when combined with deep purple curtains.

OPPOSITE This group shows the essence of a colour scheme that weaves like a magical thread through a room to pull furniture, fabrics and accessories together and create the atmosphere you want.

# pastel pink

**This pink is very, very sweet**, so be careful
not to overdo it – too much can be sickly! It is a pale
version of crimson, and, like crimson, it contains a touch
of cool blue, edging it towards mauve, which becomes
most apparent if it is used with shades of violet or
lavender. The rather feminine character of this pink
makes it a favourite for floral chintz fabrics.

  To keep it looking fresh, use it with an equal amount
of white, or let it share the limelight with pale lemon
yellow or mint green. For a more sophisticated look,
wash it over walls and use a pale, matt grey-green for
the woodwork.

# create **sweet delights**
## with **ice-cream** colours

OPPOSITE Create a nostalgic
haze with these romantic
pink curtains.

LEFT The luscious pink
combines well with grey-
green eucalyptus foliage.

BELOW The glass dish in the
foreground of this group
gives a cooling violet cast
to all the shades of pink
and white in this table setting,
creating a fresh, romantic
floral arrangement.

67

# pink windows

**These pinks are chalky pastels** which look good in each other's company, so mix powder blue, pale lemon and pistachio green together for a youthful colour scheme. Look out for new paints based on distemper (tempera), which will match the colour and the texture of real sherbet by drying to a soft chalky bloom. These are the perfect colours for a nursery or a seaside holiday home where the emphasis is strictly on having fun.

# strawberry cream

**This is the most delicious shade of pink**, which is made by mixing small amounts of scarlet with lots of creamy white. As a strawberry ripens, it turns from green to white, then yellow before finally becoming bright and juicy scarlet; when scarlet is used to make pink, the yellow in it re-emerges to warm and soften the colour. The resulting pink is a joy to live with.

Strawberry cream is a favourite colour for the exterior of thatched cottages in Suffolk, England, where it starts out as a bright pink but is soon faded by the sun, wind and rain. In country interiors it can be applied as a colour wash to give a traditional plaster pink, which suits antique furniture and fabrics very well.

OPPOSITE Pink succeeds in bringing a warm atmosphere into a potentially cold, minimalist space.

BELOW Harmonious shades of burgundy, brown and pink contrast with cool green.

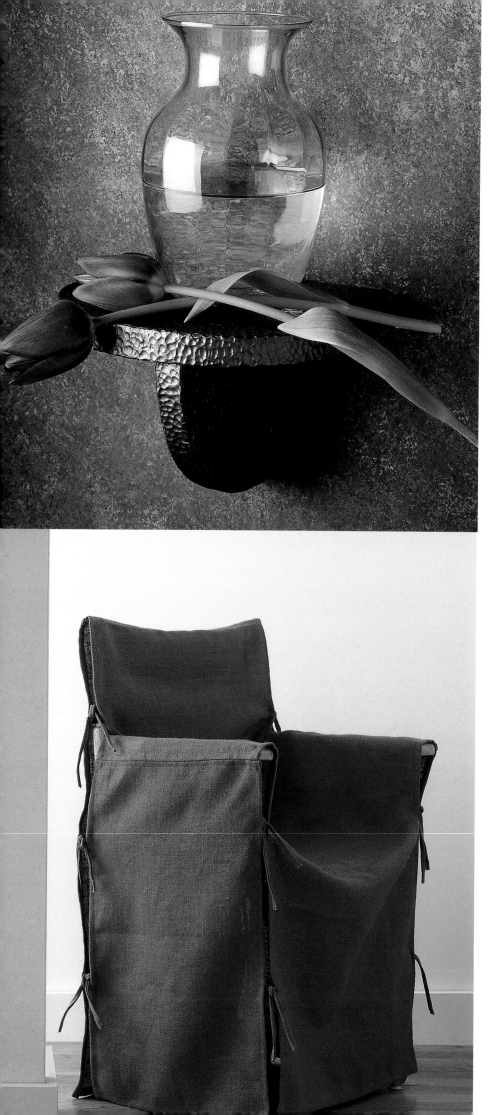

# vivid
# violet

**The colour violet** absorbs light, and it has depth and intensity. It is, however, completely altered by the proximity of other colours, red making it look more purple, while blue turns it to indigo. At its purest, violet is best used as an accent or part of a pattern rather than as a solid block of wall colour. Diluted with white, it produces lavender shades, which are easier to live with and look great with other tints, such as warm pink, grey and primrose yellow. Violet's complementary colour is a bright butter yellow, and together these provide the strongest light–dark colour contrast.

ABOVE LEFT The stark pewter combines well with the richly coloured tulip.

LEFT Colours as strong as this look fantastic against plain white walls and polished wooden floors.

OPPOSITE Set these beautiful beaded picture frames, in shades of blue, purple and violet, against a rich background.

# purple passion

**Historically, this rich colour** has been associated with royalty, high rank and the Christian church. The Romans used rare shellfish to make purple dyes, and the colour was beloved by Victorians. Aniline dyes, invented in the mid-19th century, made purple accessible to all, and it became popular for home furnishings. It did not come back into favour until the purple craze of the 1960s, when it was used in lurid combinations with orange or shocking pink.

Adding purple accessories to a room can instantly make it seem more luxurious. Look out for North African textiles, on which purple is used in unexpected combinations, such as rust, orange, red and black. A rug in these shades can be a good starting point for a colour scheme.

ABOVE This heart-shaped purple cushion gives a romantic touch to an elegant chair.

OPPOSITE Rough matt textures, give purple an up-to-date edge, while nature provides a wealth of matching blooms.

# star roller blind

### You Will Need

Matt emulsion (latex)
paints in purple and yellow
Acrylic scumble glaze
Paint mixing container
Medium paintbrush
Plain white roller blind
Natural sponge
Marker pens in black and gold
Paper
Scissors
13cm/5in square of high density
sponge, such as upholstery
foam (foam rubber)
Craft knife and cutting mat
Old plate
Bradawl
Brass screw eye
Blind-pull or tassel

Add a colour wash of purple to a plain white blind, then use its complementary colour, golden-yellow, to add the sun and stars. Use a gold pen for the outlines and match it with a gold tassel pull.

1 Mix some purple emulsion (latex) paint with acrylic scumble glaze. Lay the blind on a flat surface. Dip a natural sponge into the paint and wipe the colour over the blind. Allow to dry.

2 Draw the sun-star design freehand on to a piece of paper and cut it out. Carefully trace the shape on to a piece of high density sponge and cut out.

3 Press the sponge into the paint and then on to the blind. Outline each shape and draw in the details using a gold marker pen. Make a hole in the centre of the lower batten using a bradawl, and screw in a small brass eye. Attach a decorative blind-pull or tassel.

# blue

Everyone has experienced the clarity of a bright blue sky on a summer's day and the deep, endless blue of the night sky. Blue absorbs light and creates distance. In the landscape, blue is the colour of the distant mountains, the sea and the sky – and when we use blue on our walls the space expands. Historically, blue pigments were derived from semi-precious stones, metallic oxides and the plants, indigo and woad. All shades of blue can now be manufactured from chemicals, and the range available for decorators gets wider all the time. The colour is often associated with passive emotions and in the past was thought to have the power to drive away evil.

"the bright sky blue of the Mediterranean
appears youthful,rural and full of joy"

# blue palette

One of the three primary colours, blue ranges from cool, green-tinged turquoise through to warm,
comforting mauve. The colour is often described by the name of the place, which helps to conjure
up a particular mood – Mediterranean or Swedish, for example. These blues will also help to create
a mood when used in decorating. The bright sky blue of the Mediterranean appears youthful, rural
and full of joy, while the pale Swedish grey-blue is calm and reflective. Blue's complementary is
orange, and it harmonizes well with green and violet.

BELOW **Navy blue and white makes a
classic combination.**

BELOW **Re-create a summer's day
with a royal blue table setting.**

BELOW **Prussian blue wood-graining
creates an unusual bathroom floor.**

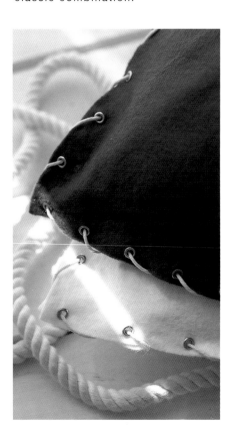

ABOVE Lilac blue fish give a lovely watery effect.

ABOVE Lavender blue towels are enhanced by a touch of white.

ABOVE A chalk blue colour wash makes a perfect backdrop.

BELOW Sky blue panelling looks great with fake fur and chrome.

BELOW Aqua blue glass droplets give a magical, watery feel.

BELOW Turquoise accessories are perfect for the bathroom.

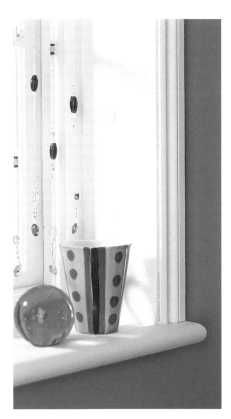

# navy blue

**The colour navy** can be so dark that it takes bright daylight to distinguish between it and black, yet it carries none of black's gloomy connotations. Navy blue is crisp, smart, efficient, positive and altogether shipshape.

Navy is seldom seen without its partner, bright white, which our eyes seem to need as reference to confirm that this dark colour is, indeed, a shade of blue. A mixture of ultramarine, cobalt and black, navy blue is available in a wide range of shades, but the colour always retains a pure blue depth that evokes the sky at night.

Navy's complementary colour is yellow-orange, which is why gold blazer buttons always look so striking against the dark fabric.

LEFT Deep navy blue fabric, folded and sewn into textured panels, creates an unusual lampshade.

# navy panelling

An inspired way to introduce both colour and texture to an otherwise plain wall is to paint inexpensive timber battens before attaching them to the wall. You'll need to mark the positions of the battens precisely on the wall.

**You Will Need**

| | |
|---|---|
| Wood battens | Spirit level |
| Pencil | Drill, with masonry and |
| Saw | wood bits |
| Paintbrush | Rawl plugs |
| Emulsion (latex) paint | Wood screws |

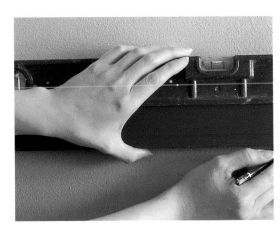

1 Measure the height and width of the wall, to make sure you have equal spacing right up the wall. Cut the wood battens to the required length.

2 Paint the battens on three sides. Use a spirit level to mark the guideline for the first strip. Drill holes in the wall and insert rawl plugs. Drill holes in the wood and then screw the strip in place. Mark the positions for the next wood strip; the space between the strips needs to be absolutely even.

# royal blue

**Royal blue is a bright, true blue**, the familiar colour that appears with red and white on the Union Flag and the primary colour that is so often used alongside yellow and red in children's decorating schemes. Designers of children's toys, books and clothing use this blue because it is the one we recognize first when we learn our colours. It is also the colour of a pattern glaze used on the famous Royal Danish porcelain. It carries positive associations and has a freshening effect when it is introduced in a room as cushions, throws, upholstery or curtains. When it is used next to primaries the effect is harsh and unsophisticated, but it works well in modern settings with its complementary orange, natural wood and a lot of white.

OPPOSITE Fresh blue-and-white gingham ribbon tied in a pretty bow turns a stack of towels into a style statement.

THIS PAGE Blue-and-white patterns can be mixed at will, because the combination of the two will always give a co-ordinated look. Grape hyacinths add a natural touch.

# prussian blue

**The distinctive dark blue** with a violet cast was first manufactured early in the 18th century from a mixture of animal blood burned with alum. Strong blues had previously been very expensive to produce and really only used in paintings, but this new production method was cheaper and the colour became extremely fashionable in house decorating. It has sophistication and looks wonderful alongside straw yellow, dull silver and natural wood. Avoid using it with bright colours, because the contrast will be too strong, and if you want white next to it, choose a white that has been toned down with burnt umber to make it mellower and warmer.

Prussian blues, in a range of light and dark shades, can be found among the historic colour ranges of speciality paint dealers. The colour looks marvellous when used matt on woodwork in a period home or as small areas of bold, dark colour on the walls of a modern room.

OPPOSITE **Deep Prussian** blues enliven this mosaic but still harmonize with the other blues and shades of green.

BELOW **The Prussian blue** upholstery and the mosaic, with shades of grey, give a cool, contemporary look.

# sophisticated
and elegant **slate** blue

87

# ribbon café curtain

Dress up a small window by making this luxurious striped curtain from ribbons in different shades of blue instead of ordinary fabric. Rows of shiny blue and green glass beads add extra sparkle to the satin, and the larger beads make a pretty hem and add weight so that the ribbons hang evenly.

1 Cut the ribbons to the finished length of the curtain plus 4cm/1 in . Trim one end of each ribbon length into a decorative point.

3 Fold over 5mm/ in then another 2.5cm/1in along the top edge to make a casing, and tack. Handstitch small glass beads along each seam.

2 Lay out the ribbons in a repeating pattern, alternating satin and chiffon, to fit the width of the window. With a matching thread and a small zigzag stitch, join the ribbons together. End each seam 7.5cm/3in from the bottom.

4 Thread a large plastic bead on to the end of each satin ribbon. Machine-stitch the casing and thread the tension rod or curtain wire through it to hang the curtain.

# lilac

**Lilac, a warm blue** with a rosy cast, is restful to the eye. The colour's name comes from the flowers of the lilac tree, and this is the image it conjures up. One superstition associated with the lilac is that the flowers will bring bad luck if they are brought into the house, but the blooms are so lovely that the tradition is often overlooked. Follow nature's example and use the colours together for a fresh summer look. Lilac can be used to create a tranquil mood with a limited palette of tonally similar shades of pale grey, pink and brown.

warm **lilac** creates
a **tranquil** mood

OPPOSITE Fluffy lilac towels, lotions and
lace arranged for bathtime meditation.

LEFT A stunning arrangement of deep lilac-
coloured hyacinths.

ABOVE Mosaic tiles in tones of lilac and
deeper blues are enhanced by stones.

# lilac dreams

**White walls are given the palest of pale lilac** colour washes before broad stripes are applied in a transparent lilac glaze to give the impression of a wall covered with voile. The border of triangles below the picture rail is easily added using a cardboard template and masking tape. A similar but more natural effect can be created by giving wooden walls a lilac colour wash.

# lavender

**Lavender blue is a calm**, meditative colour, which brings a tranquil atmosphere. The sight of a field of lavender in full bloom against a bright blue sky on a sunny day is not to be missed and is completely unforgettable. This blue prefers the company of its neighbours, blue and green, to its complementary yellow. Sage green, cream, dull silver and sky blue will enhance its calming properties.

THIS PAGE Lavender, cream and black create a serene but sophisticated look in a living room.

OPPOSITE Heart-shaped lavender bags, tied to an elegant chair, capture a romantic mood.

# embossed frame

**You Will Need**

Wooden frame
Cardboard
Felt-tipped pen
Scissors
Tape
Sheet of tin
Centre punch
Hammer
Tin snips
Protective gloves (optional)
Chisel
Ridged paint scraper
Copper nails

Tin is a soft metal that can be easily decorated, using a centre punch or a blunt chisel to create dots and lines. Keep your punched design simple and graphic because too much fine detail will get lost when the design is finally punched out.

1 Lay the wooden frame on a piece of cardboard and draw around the outline with a felt-tipped pen. Add extra length to the outside edges and around the centre to allow for turnings. Cut out the template with scissors. Tape the cardboard template on to a sheet of tin. Mark the corners using a centre punch and hammer, and mark the straight lines with a felt-tipped pen.

3 Lay the wooden frame on the tin and use a ridged paint scraper to coax the metal up the sides of the frame. Turn the frame over and push down the metal edges in the centre, again using the ridged scraper. Cut both strips of tin, each 20 x 2cm/8 x ⁄in Snip at the halfway mark and fold at a 90 angle.

2 Cut out the tin shape with tin snips (wear protective gloves to protect your hands from the sharp edges of the tin). Using a hammer and chisel, cut through the centre of the frame in a diagonal line then use the tin snips to cut out the remaining sides and open it out into a square.

4 Nail the strips to the inner edge of the frame, using copper nails. Hammer nails along the outer edges for the frame. Draw a freehand feather design on the tin frame. Use a blunt chisel and hammer to press the design on to the tin in straight lines. Clean the tin with polish and a soft cloth.

# chalk blue

**Chalk blue is a matt pastel colour**, made by softening any shade of bright blue by the addition of white. These blues feel warm and welcoming, and they are the ideal way to give a bedroom or bathroom a feminine look without resorting to a clichéd colour such as pink. The colour's character is enhanced when it is used with a matt finish, and the very best results are achieved with distemper (tempera) paint, which dries to a powdery bloom that intensifies the chalky nature of the colours. As colours mixed with white are more compatible, you won't go wrong if you limit your colour scheme to other pastels.

# warm and **welcoming** **chalk** blues

OPPOSITE Woodwork of mellow cream is the perfect contrast to rich chalk blue.

LEFT Restricting the colour scheme to chalk blue and white gives the room a calm, harmonious atmosphere.

BELOW Deep chalk blue has been used with cream and gold, with an accent of deep purple anemones, to create a sophisticated effect.

# sky blue

**To describe a colour as sky blue** is to look on the bright side, for this is the blue of the sky on an early summer's morning, holding the promise of fine, warm weather and good times to come. The same optimism we feel when we throw open the shutters and see a clear sky is conveyed when we decorate with this colour. It is also the blue associated with baby boys, forget-me-nots and faded denim jeans.

Sky blue is hardly ever out of place. In bright or dull company it will retain its clarity, so feel free to use it with primaries, pastels or neutrals.

ABOVE These walls have the look of a summer afternoon sky streaked with vapour trails.

OPPOSITE Distressed sky blue shutters are given a lavender cast by the proximity of these fantasy flowers.

# aqua blue

**Aqua means water**, and the colour's name describes a wide range of watery blue-greens. The colour has a restful, calm character, which is best projected when it is used in a combination of harmonious tints and tones. Like water, it can reflect light, a quality much prized in countries in the far northern hemisphere. It can often be seen in elegant Swedish interiors alongside off-white, with highlights of pale gold and against natural bleached pine floors.

THIS PAGE **Create a nautical feel with shades of aqua blue combined with crisp, white cotton.**

# restful, calming
## colours of the sea

LEFT The pale aqua walls of the bathroom are a subtle, sophisticated backdrop for the plaster mirror frame and star motifs.

BELOW Aqua has been used as a pale wash on the walls and as a darker, translucent wood stain on the floor. The horse motif was stamped on to white wood stain.

**The colour takes its name** from the opaque semi-precious stone associated with the Navajo people of North America, who make exquisite jewellery from the stone and silver. This is the blue-green of Egyptian murals and tropical seas, a light colour in tone and mood, most often used in bathrooms, but equally effective in a garden room that gets a lot of natural sunlight.

Turquoise is a sunny colour, which can take strong contrasts, such as burnt orange, shocking pink or brick red, but control the impact by using plenty of white between them.

# turquoise

To keep turquoise cool, use it with a range of blues and greens and the effect will be restful on the eyes.

# Egyptian murals and **tropical** seas

ABOVE LEFT Brilliant shocking pink flowers present the liveliest contrast with the turquoise-coloured vase, and other shades of the colour appear in the patterned table.

LEFT Turquoise and silver baubles cleverly create a link between the cushion cover and the shades of blue on the wall and curtain.

# decorated frame

Wood-graining is quite easy to do and the effect is startlingly realistic when you use the right tool. Two shades of turquoise have been used to change an ordinary window frame into something eye-catching.

## You Will Need

Sandpaper
Pale blue-green
vinyl silk paint
Decorator's paintbrush
Matt emulsion (flat
latex) paint
Water-based scumble

Heart grainer or rocker
Gloss acrylic varnish
Varnishing brush
Star stencil
Masking tape
Stencil brush
Acrylic frosting varnish

1 Sand the window frame then apply pale blue-green vinyl silk paint and leave to dry. For the glaze, mix one part deep blue-green emulsion (latex) to six parts scumble and apply. Draw the heart grainer or rocker across the glazed surface and leave to dry, then varnish the whole frame.

2 Make sure that the glass is clean, and then attach the stencil with masking tape. Using a stencil brush, apply the frosting evenly through the stencil. Remove the stencil before the varnish dries completely.

# green

Nature's colour of growth and hope, green is one of the primary colours of light. Historically, green pigment has come from the mineral malachite, from verdigris (the patina on the surface of copper) and even from highly toxic arsenic. Green is said to assist relaxation, concentration and meditation, all of which require a focused state of mind. The Georgians used a lot of pea green next to off-white, while Victorians preferred the more sombre olive green. Until fairly recently green was used on walls in only a pale, tinted form, but in the last decade or so ethnic influences have encouraged bolder attitudes towards home colour, and we can now buy green in wonderfully vibrant shades of lime, viridian, grass and emerald.

"nature's colour of growth,
hope and regeneration"

# green palette

A glance across open countryside or even around a garden will reveal the incredible variety that exists in shades of green. A mixture of equal quantities of pure blue and yellow produces a bright grassy green, but as more yellow is added the colour turns to spring green, vibrant lime and eventually cool lemon. When more blue is added we get pine, sea green and viridian. Each of these shades can be varied by using a mixture of more specific or subtle blues and yellows.

BELOW Bottle green provides an elegant look for a modern topiary.

BELOW Grass green carries feelings of straightfoward happiness.

BELOW An olive green wreath is a sophisticated choice.

ABOVE Sea green hearts look cool and inviting against chalk blue.

BELOW A white backdrop captures the richness of leaf green.

ABOVE Lime green has a bold, fresh and ultimately irresistible look.

BELOW Moss green describes the texture as much as the colour.

ABOVE Lemon green creates a light, airy and fresh ambience.

BELOW Lichen green is a soft, natural yellow-green.

# bottle green

**A deep, dark and dramatic colour**, bottle green can look almost black in a dimly lit room. For this reason, good lighting is most important if you are considering using it as a wall colour. This is the colour of medieval velvet robes, wine bottles and ivy creeping across a brick wall. Bottle green looks smart with cream, and the two fade elegantly alongside each other. White is not so forgiving, however, and needs to be kept pristine to maintain the sharp, fresh contrast. For a brighter look, combine bottle green with earthy rusts or peachy orange.

rich, **opulent** shades of **bottle** green

RIGHT A glass bottle and lampshade show the many different shades of bottle green revealed by the addition of light.

OPPOSITE ABOVE Creamy whites combine with light bottle greens to create the freshest of displays.

OPPOSITE BELOW This decorative plait has a traditional country look.

# grass green

**You would have to live in a desert** not to recognize grass green, which is, literally, the colour of a freshly mown summer lawn. It carries with it feelings of optimism, confidence and happiness, which makes it a good colour choice for children's rooms. This shade of green is often used for garden or conservatory furniture, perhaps because it looks so good in natural light and surrounded by other shades of green. Green has been called an "appetite colour" because it can trigger thoughts of food. This is why it is a popular choice in restaurants and is ideal for dining areas in the home. Team it with buttercup yellow and white for a fresh, summer-meadow effect or with sky blue and waxed bare wood to give a relaxed country feel.

OPPOSITE LEFT A flat green wall is the perfect backdrop for this very pretty pale grey marble table, which has been set with lemon green china and delicate glass-beaded candlesticks.

OPPOSITE RIGHT Green provides just the right feelings of freshness, youthfulness and fun in a family kitchen.

THIS PAGE The addition of a plain beaded throw gives this grass green room a relaxed, country feel.

# citrus fruit bowl

**You Will Need**

Soft pencil

Tracing paper

Stencil card (cardboard)

Craft knife or scalpel

Cutting mat

Plain fruit bowl

Masking tape

Yellow chinagraph pencil

Water-based ceramic paint:
citrus green, mid-green,
dark green and yellow

Artist's paintbrushes

Paint palette

Acrylic varnish (optional)

The combination of citrus yellow and green give a fresh, new look to a plain, china bowl. The limes are painted in an energetic freehand style and they look terrific adorning this fruit bowl, making this the liveliest centrepiece ever to grace your table.

1 Draw a freehand lime on to tracing paper and transfer it to stencil card (cardboard).Cut out the lime stencil using a sharp craft knife or scalpel and a cutting mat.

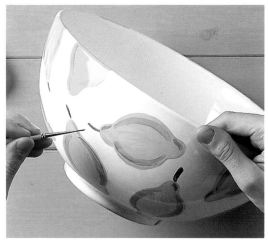

3 Add mid-green highlights to the fruits and allow the paint to dry. Paint a stalk at the end of each lime in dark green. Let the paint dry.

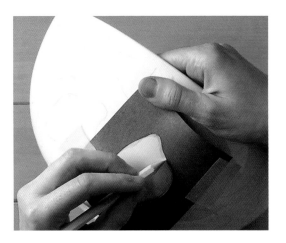

2 Attach the stencil to the bowl with masking tape. Draw inside the stencil on to the bowl using a yellow chinagraph pencil. Repeat to draw several limes all over the bowl. Fill the limes with citrus paint.

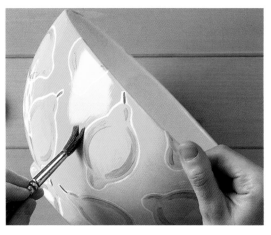

4 Paint the background yellow, leaving a thin white outline around each lime. Paint on varnish or bake the bowl in the oven according to the paint manufacturer's instructions.

# olive green

**The colour is described perfectly by its name**, which immediately summons up mental images of bowls filled with glossy green olives. Olive green is a useful and versatile colour, and it adapts easily to any mood you wish to create. Used with gold, for instance, it proclaims opulence and grandeur, but alongside golden-yellow it has its roots firmly in the rainforest. In the wrong surroundings it can fade into the background and look rather dull, but it can also be a stylish choice for a sophisticated modern room.

Both the Arts and Crafts and the art nouveau movements favoured olive green in their designs, and it was seen again in the 1970s Victorian revival. These days olive green is popular once again, but is more likely to appear as a foil for brighter colours in ethnic-style décor.

ABOVE Texture has a major effect on olive green, as can be seen in the way the glossy glaze on this earthenware storage jar illuminates the colour.

OPPOSITE Olive green is a good colour for floors, and the stencilled pattern used here is practical, yet pretty enough to banish any military associations.

bowls filled with **glossy** green **olives**

# sea green

**The name encompasses a range of colours** as wide as the ocean, from the bright blue-green of shallow water on the shoreline of the Mediterranean to the pale watery green of the ice-bound Arctic. Sea green is easy on the eye and is infinitely adaptable, looking cool or warm depending on the rest of the colour scheme. It is a colour that looks good outdoors in bright light where it actually improves as it fades.

# distressed wall

## You Will Need

Light, medium and
dark shades of soft
green and white silk-
finish emulsion
(satin finish latex)
paint (buy a dark
shade and mix it with
white to make the
light and medium
shades)
Large and medium
decorator's
paintbrushes
Medium shade of soft
green matt emulsion
(flat latex) paint
Tissue paper
Acrylic scumble
Stippling brush
Clean cotton rag

Frottage is an unusual and effective way to achieve a change of texture on a wall. It is not difficult to do and looks good on a wall divided by a dado (chair) rail. The colour and texture of the finished wall give an impression of verdigris, a naturally occurring patina on weathered copper.

1 Paint the upper part of the wall with two coats of light green silk-finish paint, leaving each to dry. Dilute the matt (flat) green paint with about 20% water. Brush this on to a section of the wall.

2 Immediately press a sheet of tissue paper over the entire surface except for a narrow band adjacent to the next section you will be working on. Work on a manageable area at a time.

3 Carefully peel back the tissue paper to reveal most of the base colour. Brush on two coats of medium green silk-finish paint over the textured wallpaper below the dado (chair) rail, leaving each to dry. If the wallpaper is new, it may bubble, but it will shrink back when dry.

4 Mix dark green silk finish with acrylic scumble in a ratio of one part paint to six parts scumble. Brush this glaze on to a section of the wallpaper.

5 Immediately dab over the wet glaze with a stippling brush to eliminate brushmarks and even out the texture.

6 Wipe a cotton cloth gently over the stippled glaze to remove it from the raised area of the wallpaper. Complete the wall section by section. Paint the dado rail with white paint, leave to dry and brush on the green glaze.

# lime green

## Bright, acid lime green on walls

is part of the colour revival that has been inspired and encouraged by the current media fascination with interior decorating. Empowered by television and magazines, people have been released from convention and given the confidence to choose brighter, bolder colours to make a statement – and lime green certainly does that!

Lime green is cool – in every sense of the word – and can be reinforced with other bold colour choices, such as cobalt blue, chocolate brown, burnt orange, shocking pink, deep purple, gold and aluminium. If you like the colour but don't want it to dominate, paint the walls white and add accents of lime and other hot colours with the soft furnishings. Smart fittings such as aluminium rails keep the look sharp and fresh.

## invigorate
your home with **zesty** lime

OPPOSITE Lime green walls and brilliant orange crockery bring instant sunshine to a kitchen.

ABOVE A mellower shade of lime green is used with a chic blend of natural materials.

# lemon green

**Lemon green, a paler, less intense** version of lime, has a name that conjures up the new, unripe fruit, and its delicacy is best captured when it is used in a translucent form. A good wall effect can be achieved by painting a basecoat of yellow then brushing over a tinted blue-green glaze. This will keep the colour light and add to its reflective quality.

Voile or muslin drapes in lemon green will cool a room without blocking all traces of the sunshine outside, and they are the perfect complement to each other, like a pitcher of lemonade and a sunny afternoon.

BELOW Lemon green gives a fresh and inviting look to walls.

OPPOSITE In warm, clever lighting, lemon green walls create a summery ambience.

# leaf green

**Leaf green is a colour** that originates in nature. Individual associations vary according to the climate, but this is usually the green of perfect, mature leaves before they fade or take on their autumnal tints. A glance at a garden will show nature's variety, but, as a paint colour, a convincingly natural leaf green has always been quite difficult to mix. Dilution with white tends to flatten the colour and rob it of its life, but clever mixing or the use of a glaze over a flat colour will go some way towards capturing its luminosity. Go the whole way and use leaf green with other shades seen in nature – earthy brown, bleached wood and rust or other deeper greens. Pale creamy yellow or icy pale blue are good background colours, and red ochre, its complementary, provides the strongest contrast.

ABOVE LEFT A garden chair gets a witty interpretation with textured turf and cheerful daisies.

LEFT The pattern on these vivid green curtains perfectly echoes the leaves of the plant, giving a summery feel.

# place mat

These stylish place mats are very easy to make and add a contemporary look to the dinner table. The smaller, gently curving flower shape could be used to make coasters with napkins tied in co-ordinating colours.

1     Make a template for the place mat then draw around the template on to the manilla cardboard. Make a pattern in the same way for the smaller inside shape and draw it on to the other colour of the card. Cut out both shapes using a craft knife and a cutting mat.

2     Draw the curved border line on to the base card in pencil. Apply a fine line of glue, following the drawn line, then carefully stick the flat cord over the glue line. Cut and butt up the cord ends where they meet. Glue the inside shape in place within the curved border.

# the natural touch

**Be inspired by the natural world** and create a fresh look that is wholly up to date. The key to success lies in the plants, colours and materials you choose. Houseplants pass in and out of fashion: an aspidistra is definitely Victorian, cheese and spider plants were popular in the 1970s, and the current preference is for sculptural plants, such as clipped topiary or large succulents, to go with the modern look.

Textures of natural materials, such as rope, cane, hessian (burlap), wood, slate and leather, blend harmoniously, and their natural colouring needs little more than the right plants, a wooden floor and a pale, warm colour on the walls.

# moss green

**Moss is nature's soft green velvet carpet**
for woodland floors, and the name describes the texture as
much as it does the colour. Moss green has freshness
without fragility and looks good in large rooms with high
ceilings or on sweeping staircases. It is a popular colour
for carpets and sumptuous fabrics, such as velvets and
silks, which drape well and catch the light.

1 Cut both colours of twine into equal lengths and knot together. Secure the cup hook into the chuck of a hand drill and loop the twine through at one end, securing it over a door handle or clamp at the other. Turn the drill until the twine is tightly spun. Release the clamped end and attach to the cup hook, twisting to make a tight cord.

2 Drill a hole in the finial from top to bottom, glue the outside and wind the brown twine around it. Rotate the finial on a knitting needle to avoid overhandling. Cut even lengths of green twine and tie in the middle with twine. This can then be tied to the cord.

3 Liberally apply glue to the top of the skirt and thread the cord through the hole in the finial. Pull so the top of the skirt sits inside the finial. Trim the tassel to an even length.

# key ring

This generously sized tassel, with its skirt of green garden twine, makes an impressive key ring. Worked over a curtain pole finial, the tassel uses the simplest of techniques to stunning effect. The striped cord is made using two different colours of twine.

**You Will Need**

Twine in 2 colours
Scissors
Cup hook
Hand drill
Clamp (optional)
Drill with wood bit
Curtain pole finial
Thick knitting needle
Instant bonding glue
Glue spreader
Mounting board or
wood, 20 x 28cm/
8 x 11in

# lichen green

**Lichen describes a soft, silvery green** with a yellow cast. It takes its name from a strange compound of fungus and algae that appears on stones, walls and trees. It is a beautiful, soft, muted colour, which can match many different moods. The silver within it is cool and hard, its green element provides softness, and the yellow gives it warmth and life. These characteristics can either be brought into focus or subdued by your choice of surrounding colours and style of accessories.

An ideal colour for subdued northern light, lichen green is perfect for a Scandinavian-style room.

THIS PAGE Crushed velvet
ribbons in lichen green
add a touch of luxury to a
plain bed throw. The
colour is also picked up,
in a slightly darker shade,
in the cushion.

OPPOSITE The pale lichen
green wall colour looks
mellow and tranquil in the
subdued natural sunlight.

# white

Purists may argue that white is not a colour, but it is recognized and described as one by all who use it. Leonardo da Vinci proclaimed white to be the "first of all simple colours", and we associate it with cleanliness, purity and light. White is the lightest, most reflective and expansive of all colours and is associated with chastity and innocence. It illuminates other colours and brings them to life without detracting from or influencing them in any other way. There are thousands of variations of white, and the human eye is adept at recognizing many of them. Choosing white for your walls is not as easy as it used to be as the range of whites available to the decorator grows wider all the time.

"we associate white with cleanliness, purity, innocence and light"

# white palette

Just as a heavy snowfall redefines a familiar landscape, a coat of white paint appears to change the proportions of a room. White can be used to highlight architectural features, such as plaster mouldings, when set against another colour, or it can just as easily hide unwanted features. If everything is painted white you get a "blank canvas" effect.

Black and white create the strongest light–dark contrast, but the effect can be too stark and require the addition of other colours for life and warmth.

BELOW Snow white gives a dazzling fresh, crisp white.

BELOW Ivory white diffuses the sunlight in this beautiful curtain.

BELOW China tableware in butter cream provides an elegant touch.

ABOVE Black and white create a sophisticated contrast.

BELOW Decorated natural fabric makes an interesting wall hanging.

ABOVE Clear glass, like water, reflects light as white.

BELOW Shells and stones give this box a sculptural elegance.

ABOVE Silver and white create a cool, contemporary look.

BELOW Wooden lime-washed floors make a room seem more spacious.

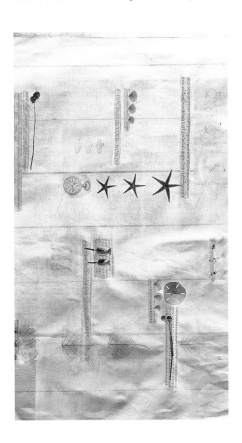

# snow white

**This is the most reflective of all whites**, capable of dazzling and disturbing the eyes. It is also the most popular, versatile, useful and least expensive paint on the market. This is the paint to reach for when you move into a new house or apartment and want to start afresh by eliminating every trace of the previous occupant's decorating disasters. It will allow you to see the proportions and make decorating decisions with clarity.

You may love your white walls and never want to change them, but if you do choose to apply colour, snow white is the ideal undercoat because it reflects the top coat's colour back at itself to give it maximum intensity.

OPPOSITE White walls, soft voile bedding and natural wood give this room a sense of elegant tranquillity.

THIS PAGE Chalky walls, starched cotton and shiny china surround this wonderful flower arrangement.

# ivory white

**Ivory is a mellow white**, easier on the eyes and more flattering to the complexion than bright white. Natural ivory yellows with age, and the name is applied across a range of warm, pale shades of white. Perhaps our most familiar visual reference for the colour would be a piano, where black ebony and white ivory make up the keys. The combination can be used to dramatic effect when decorating, and a black and ivory white checkerboard floor, immortalized in the paintings of Dutch interiors, has remained popular for hundreds of years.

Ivory walls, carpeting and soft furnishings are totally impractical in rooms used by young children, so the choice is both sophisticated and extravagant. This has made ivory a favourite with upmarket interior designers, who mix it with natural materials and fabrics, such as muslin, linen, leather, bleached and waxed wood, stone and rope.

While bright white suits bright sunshine, it looks chilly in a cloudy climate, but ivory reflects any incoming light and instils warmth. Use it with muted dark colours, such as Prussian blue.

OPPOSITE **The classic shape and colour of this vase make it the perfect receptacle for an elegant arrangement of ivory-coloured tulips.**

ABOVE **Fluted corrugated cardboard and woven ivory-coloured fabric have been combined to make an extremely stylish lamp.**

141

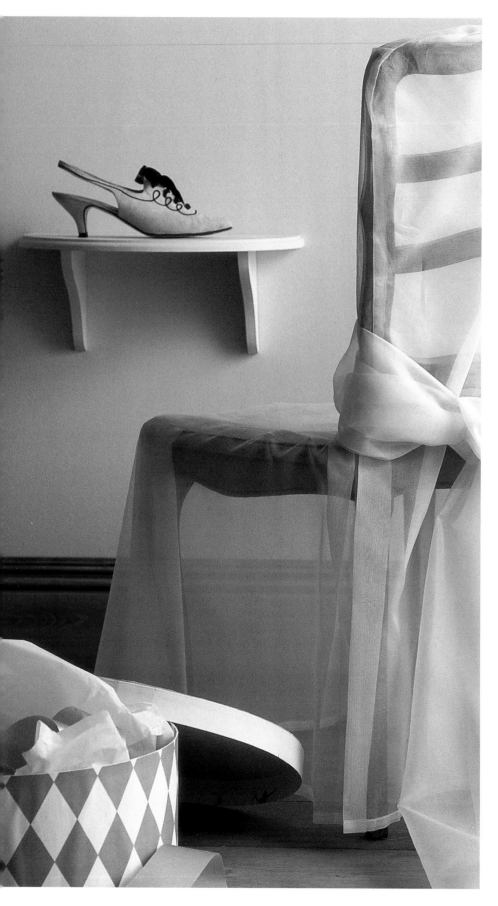

# butter cream

**This rich, yellowy cream** was the most popular colour for interior woodwork during the Edwardian period, when light colours and pretty patterns replaced the gloom of the late Victorian years. Now, however, it is most often used as part of the country-decorating palette, in which Shaker style and historic colours combine in harmonious simplicity.

Butter cream looks good in a gloss finish, making window frames and other woodwork look simply delicious. Used in this way, it looks surprisingly good with matt white walls and also combines well with most other colours. In modern living rooms and entrance halls it is a useful way to take the cold edge off minimalist styling.

LEFT **Walls clad in butter cream add a warm nostalgic feel to an interior, here enchanced by the choice of accessories.**

# bucket stool

Florist's buckets in galvanized tin are widely available in a variety of heights, and for this project the taller the bucket, the better. For a touch of milking parlour nostalgia choose a cream waffle tea towel (dish cloth) for the seat.

## You Will Need

| | |
|---|---|
| 1m/1yd heavy cord | Fabric cutting tool |
| or rope | for buttons |
| 2 florist's buckets | Waffle tea towel |
| Glue gun | (dish cloth) |
| Large self-cover buttons | Circular cushion pad |
| Material scraps for | Large sewing needle |
| buttons | Matching thread |

1 Attach the cord or rope to the top rim of one of the buckets using the glue gun. Place this bucket inside the second bucket, applying glue to its rim, then invert both buckets. Use the fabric to cover the buttons.

2 Sew the buttons through the waffle hand towel. Use the towel to cover the cushion pad. Instead of smoothing out the gathering in the fabric, accentuate it, using the buttons as a focus. Glue the pad to the bucket.

# cream

**Cream is a neutral white with a slightly yellow cast** and no trace of grey or pink, unlike the ubiquitous magnolia. Older properties will always look better painted cream than stark white because bright titanium white was a 20th-century invention, and the white pigments used before it was available yellowed naturally with age. It is a classically elegant colour. In a modern setting, cream will have a warming effect on even stark, minimalist interiors, and it is an integral part of the "new" natural colour scheme, where it mixes well with pale slate grey, stone, suede and chocolate browns. Cream is an ideal choice for this style, with its emphasis on space, light, comfort, natural materials and interesting shapes.

# black and white

**The extremes of contrast** in dark and light, black and white carry so many universally recognized associations, from chessboards and zebra skins to piano keys. Cole Porter wrote a marvellous song about a famous decorator called Elsie de Wolfe (later Lady Mendl), whose black-and-white style had a huge influence on decorating in the 1920s.

The starkness of the black–white contrast lacks warmth and is more likely to be seen in stylish galleries and offices than in a family home. To introduce warmth without adding other colours, choose polished wooden floors, textured fabrics, plants and warm lighting.

## from **chessboards** and zebra skins to **piano keys**

OPPOSITE ABOVE Fabric, draped in the Regency style, makes an elegant, sophisticated window treatment.

OPPOSITE BELOW A perfect balance of contrasts here with black and white: soft and textured.

LEFT An unusual arrangement of floor tiles creates large black crosses.

# Japanese screen

**You Will Need**
Garden trellis
Blackboard paint
Paintbrush
Heavyweight tracing
paper
Staple gun
Craft knife
Red emulsion
(latex) paint
Drill
2 screw eyes
Tape measure
Wire coat hanger
Pliers
2 picture hooks

A black-and-white window screen with a few well-chosen pieces of furniture gives this room an almost authentic Japanese look. The wooden screen is actually a simpl garden trellis, painted black and backed with semi-transparent draughtsman's tracing paper. The walls and woodwork have been painted the same creamy white colour. This screen is the perfect treatment for a minimalist room.

Paint the trellis black, and leave to dry. Paint one square red for added interest. Blackboard paint creates a perfectly matt finish, but other matt or gloss paints can be used. Staple sheets of tracing paper to the back of the trellis, and trim to ensure there are no overlaps.

Drill a very fine hole in the top of the trellis at the end of the first strut in from each end. Screw a screw eye into each hole.

Measure the length of the window to determine how long the hooks for hanging should be. The base of the screen should touch the window frame below. Cut two pieces of coat hanger wire to the correct length for the hooks. Then hang the screen on these from picture hooks.

# translucence

**The effect of light passing through an imperfectly clear material**, such as frosted glass or sheer white voile, produces an effect we call translucence. This is not a pigment, but it is the way we perceive and illustrate light. Translucence produces a softening of hard edges and a very gentle, flattering light.

This quality of translucence is best revealed when glass, or another transparent material, is surrounded by a more solid version of white or another very pale colour, so that light creates soft reflections on its surface. Muslin-shaded windows, misty window panes, floating candles in a glass bowl or a milky glaze on a wall all produce a translucent effect.

OPPOSITE Soft lighting on glass, polished silver, white muslin and petals creates a pretty, translucent effect.

ABOVE The effect of the lighted candle and floating petals is enhanced by reflections in the water and on the glass.

# molten silver

**The industrial pressed steel** look came in with high tech and the New York loft style and has refused to go away. It may have had its roots in industry, but molten silver is now one of the most popular looks for the home. Metallic finishes no longer have to be cold and hard, because you can buy convincing acrylic paints in most metal shades, and these are suitable for painting on any surface. Dull molten silver is cool in both senses of the word and can take the excitement of being mixed with vibrant colours. Go for the retro look with American diner styling or stay aloof with black, white and grey.

THIS PAGE Silver combined with white light creates a warming effect.

OPPOSITE The shine turns grey into silver. Shot silk is dressed up with a latticework of silver trimmings.

# natural fabric

**These might be called feel-good fabrics** – the linens, raffias, hemps and muslins whose irregularities we cherish because they are the very antithesis of man-made uniformity. The colours come from plants and from fibres ripened and bleached by the sun.

The natural look has come of age with the millennium, as people everywhere become aware of the need to value the planet's limited resources. Use stone, wood, glass, baskets and plants, and neutral, light-enhancing colours to create a naturally mellow environment.

BELOW Sweet dreams are guaranteed in the restful natural shades of the fresh linen sheets and a headboard softened by coils of soft rope.

TOP LEFT Each curtain tab is decorated with a woven hemp ribbon and a different dried, scented spice pod.

TOP RIGHT Cross-sections of the natural world are framed and celebrated in a beautiful hessian (burlap) curtain.

BOTTOM LEFT These loosely woven brown linen curtains reflect the essence of modern, naturally elegant style.

BELOW Golden light filtering through a woven raffia blind brings a nostalgic Robinson Crusoe look to any room.

In recent years, our need to feel in touch with nature and concerns for the environment have led to a revival of interest in natural materials. Shells and stones are perhaps an unusual decorative material for the home, but in a simple interior they can breathe life into a room. Make the most of *objets trouvés* brought back as souvenirs from trips to the seaside – collecting shells and pebbles at the beach is even more addictive if you know you are going to use them later.

# shells & stones

ABOVE LEFT Bring a touch of class and a quirky seaside style to a simple brown paper lampshade. Using pebbles worn smooth by sea-waters and picked up at the beach, you can create a work of art that is truly individual.

LEFT Pebbles, cobbles and stone have been used the world over to create beautifully classic yet hardwearing floors. The simple checkerboard design here looks stunning in its simplicity.

delight in the beauty and coolness of
**sea-washed** pebbles

# shell curtain

If you love to be beside the seaside, this is the perfect way to express that feeling. It is simple enough to make in an afternoon with a pocketful of shells, and some fine cotton sheeting.

The elegance of this curtain is easy to achieve by drilling shells and stitching them on to a curtain. Once made, simply peg it up on a piece of string with clothes pegs.

## You Will Need

Tape measure
Lightweight cotton, polycotton or muslin fabric
Scissors
Needle
Thread
Mini drill
Assorted small shells
Reusable tacky putty
Cord
Wooden clothes pegs
Screw eyes

Measure your window and cut enough fabric to cover it, allowing extra for a slight gather and seams and hems. Make up the curtain.

Drill a hole in each of the shells and then stitch the shells onto the curtain in staggered rows, approximately 7.5cm/3in apart.

Thread the cord through the holes in the wooden clothes pegs: the larger the hole, the more easily the curtain will draw back. Attach the cord to your window frame using screw eyes. Clip the pegs to the top of the curtain.

# wood

**A wood-brown and white combination** is delicious. Natural wood shades range from yellow through red to deep grey-brown, and applications of wax polish or varnish will preserve and enrich the surface of any type of wood. Because wood has always been a building material, it is impossible to imagine it looking out of place in our homes. People have a natural affinity for wood.

breathe new life into your **home** with the simple **elegance** of natural wood

As a rule, golden wood shades suit bold bright colours, while limed and bleached woods look best with pale colours. Dark woods suit cream or ethnic-style fabrics.

OPPOSITE The simple elegance of the pure white drapes provides a perfect background for an antique wooden folding chair.

ABOVE RIGHT Natural textures are provided by twisted willow, a brown glazed pot, a thick twist of rope and a woven cane chest.

RIGHT The woven twig-work and crisply starched cotton bed linen make an interesting contrast of rough brown and smooth white.

# natural tones

**The palette of natural tones** represents the recent fusion between fashion and interior design. The cool, expensive, elegant style appeared first on the catwalk, but the style was soon adopted for interiors, initially in design studios and shops but then in domestic settings. After all, the clothes look best in an appropriately stylish environment.

Natural fabrics, mixed with bare wood, glass, metal and earthenware, and the non-colours, in shades such as taupe, khaki, grey, oatmeal and white, declare allegiance to this sophisticated, uncluttered style.

# the colourful garden

Planning a garden can be just as much fun as planning an interior; you only have to know how to go about it. This section offers a wealth of ideas to provide you with anything from a quick fix of spring colour to a beautiful planting scheme for a whole border.

# using colour in the garden

The first big rule about using colour in the garden is anything goes. And second, there are some clever tricks; the best of them go like this.

You can make a garden seem longer by putting pale colours at the far end, so the space seems to filter away. And you get the opposite effect by using strong colours which bring everything right in and much closer. They hint at different dimensions. If you want to create eye-catchers, to get people to look more here than there, use snappy adjuncts like red and yellow, or blue and orange which grab the eye. But be careful. Such combinations or clashes mean you can't plant a subtle pastel beauty nearby because it won't get a look in. Instead, make it the star of its own special, quiet arrangement. All gardens need quiet areas, a kind of tension-free hum before you get on to the trumpets.

BELOW *Dahlia* 'Aylett's Gaiety' works well underplanted with rich blue forget-me-nots and grape hyacinths.

## Lighting

Try to place some star plants where they will be lit by the sun. *Molinia caerulea arundinacea* is a terrific grass that grows quite large, with a mound of 90cm (3ft) high leaves and flowering stems poking 1.5m (5ft) higher. It glows a fierce sugary-orange in the middle of autumn. If you can't find it, 'Zuneigung' is even better, like a porcupine on fire. Make sure you plant it in a big open space where it can be seen lit by the orange-gold autumn sun. The same applies to anything red (dahlias, or roses in fire-engine red such as 'Parkdirektor Riggers', which really pick up this glow), orange (kniphofias) or yellow (the flashy foliage of a liquidambar before it falls).

If you like growing cannas, go for 'Durban', with its striped foliage. They look terribly dull with the sun shining full on them, all pink and black stripes without any life at all, but when the sun is shining through the foliage they look 100 per cent better, shot with orange and green. You've also got to think about placing yellow. Back-lit yellow, with the sun shining through from behind, as through a stained glass window, is nothing like yellow with the sun blasting full frontal. The effects are totally different.

And that is one of the big points about colour. It is not fixed. For example, distance creates different tones. When you look at a red close up it has plenty of clout, but seen further away the effect is calmer, and not so "in your face".

If you place pink under a fierce overhead sun it looks washed out, but at dusk and dawn it is darker. So is pale blue. In fact if you want a blue garden, the time of day when it really stands out is early evening. That is because the eye is better at picking up blue in fading light, the very time when the light has a blue cast, which gets reflected back by anything blue. All of which means if you want blues to stand out, plant them in semi-shade. And if white is your favourite colour, it is best at twilight when it leaps out of the growing dark.

## Colour Combinations

Think of gardening as flower arranging on a big scale and you'll quickly see how it works. Nothing is grown in isolation. You can use blocks of colour like blue forget-me-nots (*Myosotis*

BELOW Green is valid as a colour in its own right as this lavish planting scheme shows.

ABOVE A fresh spring bulb display of 'Heart's Delight' tulips interplanted with *Chionodoxa luciliae*.

*sylvatica*) with yellow tulips such as 'West Point', and both colours stand out that bit more. The technique works extremely well with blue and orange, and yellow and purple. You can also use blocks of colour like purple around a few whites. You can even combine two colours to hint at an illusory third. Red and yellow give the ghost of an orange, and blues with reds suggest purple.

## Repeat Planting

You need a big garden and plenty of space to indulge in blocks of one colour. One trick is well worth copying. If you pack together various blues such as 'Perle d'Azur', the bluest clematis, and *Cerinthe major* 'Purpurascens', you inevitably look closer and closer, studying the nuances, texture and shapes. The monochrome draws you in. You can also use repeat plantings of certain colours in borders to make the eye skip along. Start with groups of three, then seven, nine and thirteen, and you build up a lively rhythm. You can also use this technique to avoid creating a garden with big, bold, separate blotches of colour. Group most of your whites together, but make sure you get scatterings of white all around to help the eye move on.

## Reflections

One of the main advantages of a big garden pond is that it can catch big reflections, muted but strong. The best you can get are the powerful reds and yellows when the foliage on Japanese maples (*Acer palmatum*), spindle trees (*Euonymus*) and tupelos (*Nyssa*) fire up their autumn show.

## Classic Combinations and Surprises

Nobody plants a garden in one go. Start with what's on sale now, then decide which colour goes best next to each plant. That's the easy bit. But if you need a white, which white? *Crambe cordifolia*, with its floaty aerial haze of tiny white flowers? Or a knee-high *Argyranthemum* with white daisy-like flowers? Or the great whoosh of scented white flowers on common jasmine (*Jasminum officinale*)? You choose. That's the first stage. The second is getting extra colours to pop up in every season. And the third stage involves mixing colour with size, shape and texture, the best example being one of the best sights in any garden – a late spring to early summer laburnum tunnel. The longer the tunnel the better, with thousands of bright yellow flowers hanging down, above your head, and stabbing out of the ground purple drumstick alliums giving bright colours, thin verticals, globes and an absolutely astonishing mass of droopy, dangly flowers.

## Extra Kinds of Colour

Flowers are key when thinking up a colour scheme, but they are not the end of the story. Coloured stems and berries are incredibly important, especially when winter puts paid to most flowers. The range is surprisingly large. If you want smart, brilliant-coloured stems, *Acer palmatum* 'Sango-kaku' is the one for red. Add the effect of the dogwoods, like the red-stemmed *Cornus alba* 'Sibirica' and *Tilia platyphyllos* 'Rubra' limes, which have a fuzz of red twigs high on top of the tree, then all you need is snow to really bring out the colours.

The best berry-bearing plants include *Callicarpa bodinieri* 'Profusion' with hundreds of tiny, shiny, lilac balls on bare winter branches, reaching about 3m (10ft) high. Grow it near *Clematis* 'Bill Mackenzie', which produces wonderful, silvery spidery seedheads when the yellow flowers are dead. For the biggest, fattest berries on a rose, get 'Scabrosa', which makes a great flowering bush with a profusion of crimson-pink blooms. *Rosa macrophylla* 'Master Hugh' has monster hips. And if you want hips high up, dangling out of trees, try the white *Rosa helenae*, 5.4m (18ft) high. Then there are hollies (*Ilex*) and the rare *Ilex ketambensis* with 2.5cm- (1in-) long berries, and *Pyracantha*, *Sorbus* and *Viburnum davidii* with its turquoise egg-shaped berries (you'll need male and female plants to get them). If you want bright, succulent berries to attract birds, grow cotoneaster for sparrows, starlings and thrushes, hawthorn (*Crataegus*) for blue tits, finches and pheasants, and holly for bullfinches, robins and waxwings. Garden colour is good for us, and it attracts the wildlife.

BELOW **A beautiful display that is easy on the eye, using purple sage, euphorbia, lavender and irises.**

# yellow

Yellow is one of the key garden colours. You can use it in great clusters in spring with daffodils (*Narcissus*) and crocuses, out on the lawn and under deciduous trees, and to jazz up the dull days of winter with mahonias and winter jasmine (*Jasminum nudiflorum*).

The value of yellow used in small groups with reds or blues is that it immediately grabs the eye. This is especially the case with mulleins such as *Verbascum olympicum* with its startling spires of flowers. You can use bright yellow in bigger groups, but because it can be overpowering on its own, be sure to include some muted tones. The range of yellow flowers is vast – from lilies that look like hummingbirds to anemones like flashes of butter. Just make sure you choose some with style.

*Lilium* 'Cover Girl'

# bright yellow

Strong yellows make striking look-at-me schemes. If you need a really dominant shrub try *Berberis* 'Goldilocks', or if you want a yellow perennial to keep the border alive and kicking into early autumn, the brilliant deep golden yellow flowers of the rudbeckias are perfect. And there is a wide range of dahlias, lilies and roses with incredible shape and style.

ABOVE Cactus dahlias, such as 'Hidalgo Climax' give a bright, punchy look to the late summer garden.

ABOVE Yarrow (*Achillea*) is indispensable in cottage and wildlife gardens, here forming drifts of vivid yellow.

ABOVE Even small daffodils such as *Narcissus* 'Rip van Winkle', 13cm (5in) high, give a colourful show.

ABOVE Black-eyed Susan (*Rudbeckia fulgida* var. *deamii*) gives a flash of yellow for a strong autumn show.

ABOVE *Rosa* 'Poulgan' makes an excellent patio rose for planting in gaps between paving on a terrace.

ABOVE Lilies are never disappointing; this smart bright yellow will give a big boost to any midsummer display.

ABOVE For a brilliant mid-spring show of golden daffodils try *Narcissus* 'Dutch Master'.

ABOVE *Halimium* x *pauanum* is an evergreen shrub, just right for the front of the early summer border.

ABOVE *Berberis* 'Goldilocks' gives a big display of tiny yellow flowers in spring, followed by dark blue fruit.

ABOVE *Tulipa kolpakowskiana* is a lovely mini tulip, 20cm (8in) high, for the rock garden or front of a border.

ABOVE *Rhododendron luteum* is really a deciduous azalea with a rich scent in late spring and early summer.

ABOVE Daffodils start flowering quite early, and *Narcissus* 'February Gold' is one of the first to bloom.

ABOVE *Iris danfordiae* is a gorgeous, tiny yellow gem, 15cm (6in) high, which flowers in early spring.

ABOVE The monkey flower (*Mimulus*) comes in plenty of smart bright colours such as this vivid yellow.

ABOVE End spring on a high with *Tulipa* 'Hamilton', which has wonderful fringed edges.

ABOVE *Anemone ranunculoides* 'Pleniflora' is a spreading perennial, which bursts into flower in spring.

# spring yellow

**This is the colour to save for spring** Use it in the biggest boldest groups of daffodils because the great absence of other colours, except green, means it rarely produces clashes. And as the first major colour of spring, it also has wonderful shock value – days of nothing, then the garden looks as if it has been doused in egg yolks. In summer, bright punchy yellows such as *Coreopsis grandiflora* or *Rudbeckia fulgida* 'Goldsturm' really pep things up.

BELOW LEFT The classic late spring mix of vivid, yellow tulips and dark blue forget-me-nots (*Myosotis*).

BELOW RIGHT *Lysimachia punctata* gives a strong show from midsummer onwards.

RIGHT Daffodils always offer a superb display of spring colour, whether in a border or in grass.

# pale yellow

Pale yellow is a highly valuable colour that adds to mellow background drifts. It is also a terrific link colour because it blends with green. Try primroses (*Primula*) and wallflowers (*Erysimum cheiri*) in spring, then enjoy honeysuckle (*Lonicera*), daylilies (*Hemerocallis*) and roses in summer. For winter, *Cornus stolonifera* 'Flaviramea' has bendy, watery-yellow shoots.

ABOVE *Dahlia* 'Clair de Lune' is a gentle pale yellow, a good contrast to stronger colours.

ABOVE *Rosa xanthina* 'Canary Bird' is a beautiful spring-flowering shrub, 3m (10ft) high and wide.

ABOVE The soft, pale yellow marigold *Tagetes* 'French Vanilla' likes a hot sunny place in the garden.

ABOVE *Osteospermum* 'Buttermilk' gives beautiful, pale yellow, daisy-like flowers all summer long.

ABOVE A big display of yellow-centred *Dahlia* 'Lilliput' makes a burst of fresh summer colour.

ABOVE *Rosa* 'Peace' is a classic rose, with soft yellow flowers and dark green, glossy leaves.

ABOVE Lilies, especially when they look this good, are key plants in any formal or cottage garden scheme.

ABOVE *Hypericum olympicum* makes a neat 30cm (12in) mound covered with star-shaped flowers.

ABOVE *Rhododendron* 'Narcissiflorum' is a good choice for a medium size garden, with scented spring flowers.

ABOVE Primroses (*Primula*) are perfect in spring, but make sure they get some shade and moist soil.

ABOVE The Chinese *Iris forrestii* blooms in early summer, and has the most exquisite flowers.

ABOVE 'Arthur Bell' is a 90cm (3ft) high, scented rose that keeps flowering all summer long.

ABOVE *Dahlia* 'Lemon Elegans' is a small semi-cactus type, absolutely essential for late summer-autumn.

ABOVE The Alpine bottlebrush (*Callistemon sieberi*) needs a sunny sheltered site.

ABOVE The daylily *Hemerocallis* 'Wind Song' produces prolific, gorgeous, creamy-yellow flowers.

ABOVE *Anthemis tinctoria* 'E.C. Buxton', with its mass of pale yellow flowers, is ideal for a free-flowing scheme.

# soft yellow

**Gardens need surprises, and yellows** make a big one, especially when you find an unexpected self-enclosed area with unobtrusive colours mixed with a few jumping-out, brasher tones. The plants that have the greatest pale yellow presence include spring tulips, particularly when planted in a huge romping mass, beautiful soft-toned roses, and best of all, mulleins (*Verbascum*). The tallest ones tend to be sulphur yellow and their fun, mad spires can hit 1.8m (6ft) by midsummer. You need at least one of them such as *Verbascum olympicum* with the far quieter, gentler 'Gainsborough', to give the scheme a bit of muscle.

FAR LEFT Mulleins, such as this *Verbascum* 'Gainsborough', are top-choice plants.

ABOVE LEFT Highlight pale yellow roses against an attractive ornamental feature.

ABOVE RIGHT A frothy spring display of white tulips ('Snowpeak' and 'Sweet Harmony') and mixed wallflowers.

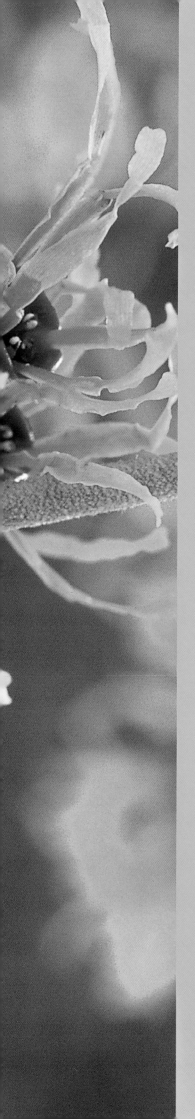

# orange

Colours don't come any hotter than orange, which is why it needs to be used judiciously. Include it in a strong, dominant hothouse display with plenty of reds and yellows, with no attempt to tone it down, or in brief occasional flashes, giving a good surprise.

One of the best oranges is *Crocosmia* 'Emily McKenzie', or *Crocosmia* 'Firebird' with a dash of red. The leaves are like thin, vertical swords, and you can plant them to flash out of shrubs like Mexican orange blossom (*Choisya ternata*). If orange sounds too intense and garish for summer, in winter it is an absolute boon, and there are plenty of excellent shrubs and trees with lashings of orange fruit and berries, such as sorbus, cotoneaster and firethorn (*Pyracantha*). The harder the berries, the less likely the birds are to eat them.

*Hamamelis* 'Jelena'

# warm orange

Orange can be used carefully to lead up to a major show of hothouse reds, or as the dominant colour and the centre of it's own vivid scheme. The flowers with the best colours tend to appear and peak in summer and autumn, and using the latter means you can certainly create end-of-season displays with plenty of marvellous clout. Always go out on a high.

ABOVE There are many annual and perennial marigolds (*Tagetes*) that enliven front of the border displays.

ABOVE Osteospermums typically have white flowers, so when you see an orange one, snap it up.

ABOVE *Rosa* 'Sweet Magic' produces large clusters of orange flowers from early summer to the autumn.

ABOVE *Rhododendron* 'Redshank' gives a deep warm colour. If you don't have acid soil, grow it in a tub.

ABOVE *Lilium davidii* can have up to 40 striking orange-red flowers on each stem, set against dark leaves.

ABOVE *Helianthemum nummularium* is a dwarf spreading shrub, making good ground cover in bright sun.

ABOVE Lion's ear (*Leonotis leonurus*) is a tender South African plant that must be brought indoors over winter.

ABOVE Dahlias are essential in any strong, vivid display, and this orange will hold its own in any group.

ABOVE 'Ellen Huston' is a prize-winning dwarf dahlia with dark foliage that does not need staking.

ABOVE The magnificent water-lily tulip (*Tulipa kaufmanniana*) and its hybrids appear in early spring.

ABOVE *Rosa* 'Warm Welcome' is a new miniature climber reaching 2.1m (7ft) high, with a mass of flowers.

ABOVE The orange daisy-like flowers of *Helenium* 'Chipperfield Orange' are ideal in hot sunny borders.

ABOVE 'Anna Ford', with its orange-red flowers and gold stamens, is a medium size rose, 1.5m (5ft) high.

ABOVE Cannas are the champions of any sub-tropical display, with big leaves and gladioli-like flowers.

ABOVE Poppies (*Papaver*) are easily grown plants that readily self-seed their way around the garden.

ABOVE *Rosa* 'Top Marks' is an exquisite miniature rose ideal for growing by patios.

# brilliant orange

**Orange is one of the brightest** garden colours. If used in huge quantities it can be completely over the top, so save it for sudden highlights. Make it really stand out by using it against a background of green foliage, especially a dark green hedge of yew (*Taxus*) or beech (*Fagus*). It also makes a lively climax to a yellow-and-red display, and since plants such as dahlias and nasturtiums (*Tropaeolum*) are going strong in these colours right to the end of summer into autumn, they guarantee the gardening year ends on a high. If you want it to go one step further, get the red-hot poker *Kniphofia uvaria* 'Nobilis', which stands out like an electrifying lamppost.

## warm and **welcoming** bright **fiery** oranges

RIGHT Flashy hothouse plants like *Crocosmia* 'Lucifer' and *Helenium* 'Waldtraut' always look best in early autumn when they're intensified by the orange cast of the sun.

FAR RIGHT TOP A terrific effect can be achieved with ordinary plants, as with these orange wallflowers and 'Queen of Night' tulips.

FAR RIGHT BOTTOM Flamboyant cannas come in all shapes and sizes, with a few special ones that you can even grow in water.

# red

Red is the key garden colour with real impact. It immediately grabs the eye, but if it is used in large numbers of plants in small gardens, it dominates and blots out everything else. Using it with other colours, especially dotted among whites, yellows, pinks and blues, creates quite beautiful contrasts. Plenty of plants offer superb reds, from hybrid tea or large-flowered bush roses that have tightly scrolled buds (climbing 'Crimson Glory' is one of the best with a gorgeous scent) to annual poppies (*Papaver*), dahlias such as 'Hillcrest Royal' and perennials such as *Potentilla atrosanguinea* 'Gibson's Scarlet'. Plenty of plants also offer dark plum-red foliage such as *Lobelia* 'Queen Victoria'. In big numbers they get a bit gloomy, so use them as a surprise among brighter flowers.

*Rosa* 'Papa Meilland'

# rich red

The reds come in a surprisingly large range, from deep dark maroon to 'in-your-face' flashy. Choosing the right background is extremely important if their effect is not to be lost. White walls in the case of climbers, and greens and whites for shrubs and perennials, are almost as important as the plants themselves.

ABOVE For an early spring red, the tiny *Tulipa linifolia* offers an excellent display of colour.

ABOVE Try swirling red ribbons of colour through a border using *Dahlia* 'Harvest Red Dwarf'.

ABOVE The new American dahlia 'Tally Ho' is a punchy dark red, excellent in vivid colour schemes.

ABOVE The fantastic scarlet *Passiflora coccinea* will thrive in a warm conservatory.

ABOVE 'Ena Harkness' is a climbing midsummer rose that rarely grows more than 4.5m (15ft) high.

ABOVE *Pelargonium* 'Happy Thought' is a terrific pot plant with crimson flowers and yellow-splashed leaves.

ABOVE The most indispensable dahlia is the bright red 'Bishop of Llandaff', with contrasting dark red foliage.

ABOVE *Rhododendron* 'James Gable' makes a great feature with its show of red flowers in the spring.

ABOVE *Rosa* 'Mister Lincoln' makes an excellent rich red for the border, and provides scores of cut flowers.

ABOVE Verbenas are essential in any display of annuals; they also come in whites, blues, mauves and pinks.

ABOVE *Camellia* 'Bob's Tinsie' is a smart, compact shrub that is covered with brilliant red flowers.

ABOVE Busy Lizzies (*Impatiens*) offer amazing colour all summer, and are just what you need to fill any gaps.

ABOVE *Dahlia* 'Willo's Surprise' has pompom-shaped wine-red flowers that grow about 90cm (3ft) high.

ABOVE *Rosa* 'Dublin Bay' is a mini climber offering shiny dark green leaves and glowing red flowers.

ABOVE 'Bob Hope' is the ideal compact camellia. Its dark red flowers go well with any bright yellow.

ABOVE For late summer to autumn hothouse schemes, you need the likes of this *Dahlia* 'Fire Mountain'.

ABOVE Tulips come in all colours from white to pink and blue, and include some startling reds.

LEFT Bright pot plants like *Pelargonium* 'Harvard' can be used on patios or in windowboxes to add splashes of colour.

RIGHT Make a strong display of rich bright reds with *Geum* 'Mrs J. Bradshaw', *Lychnis chalcedonica* and *Rosa* 'Fragrant Cloud'.

# fiery reds

**If you're going to use red**, you've got to have one or two plants in pillar box or fire engine red that take the colour up to its limit. Group a few dark reds together using plants like *Cosmos atrosanguineus*, whose flowers smell of chocolate on hot sunny days, mourning widow (*Geranium phaeum*) and *Knautia macedonica*, which produces a fantastic mass of pincushion reds all summer, then inject vermillion in the middle. If you want to keep the scarlet theme running on into late autumn, make sure that you have a Japanese maple (*Acer palmatum*) like 'Komon nishiki' or 'Matsukaze', whose leaves flare into the most extraordinary scarlet before the winter comes.

# pink

Soft pink is an excellent colour for calming down the garden, but sharp or strong pink is on the verge of being bright red. Soft pinks rarely work well in large groups because they can be extremely timid, but they are a great way of building up to something much more dramatic. Note that some pinks can change colour markedly in different lights. Soft pinks whiten out in full sun, while they gain extra richness at twilight. Also, some pink plants offer excellent scent. At the top of the list are *Viburnum* x *bodnantense*, which flowers over winter, the daphnes, especially *Daphne bholua* 'Jacqueline Postill' in late winter, and sweet peas (*Lathyrus*), lilies and roses at the height of summer. Using scented plants is an extra way of making sure that the flowers are really noticed.

*Pelargonium* 'Rollisson's Unique'

# dark pink

Rich, dark pinks come in all shapes and sizes, from low, flat ground cover giving a wide mat between large shrubs and a vista right across the garden, to taller, obtrusive shrubs that can foreshorten a view with rich colour. There's also a chance to add tall spires such as foxgloves (*Digitalis*), and some superb plants such as bougainvillea which provide a fantastic array of hues.

ABOVE *Camellia* 'Elizabeth Hawkins' is a smart bright pink that immediately perks up the garden.

ABOVE The reddish-pink flowers of *Helianthemum* 'Sudbury Red' offer a splash of colour in a rockery.

ABOVE *Clematis* 'Allanah' is well worth getting for its fantastic bright reddish-pink flowers and black anthers.

ABOVE Honesty (*Lunaria annua*) gives near purple flowers from late spring on, growing about 90cm (3ft) high.

ABOVE Foxgloves (*Digitalis*) rarely look out of place in the border, where they shoot up in summer.

ABOVE Tall, bright perennial lupins (*Lupinus*), such as this one in lipstick pink, make very good 'eye-catchers'.

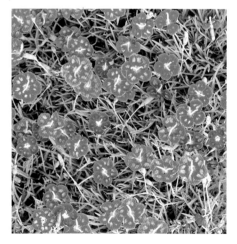

ABOVE Pinks (*Dianthus*) make super cut flowers, and give terrific displays in sunny gardens with good drainage.

ABOVE *Rhododendron* 'Hydon Dawn' is a big-value, small, compact shrub, with masses of pink flowers.

ABOVE *Rosa* 'Hansa' has large, highly scented blooms tinged reddish-violet, followed by impressive hips.

ABOVE If you've got room in your conservatory, a free-flowering bougainvillea is a must.

ABOVE Alliums offer some of the best excitement in the early summer garden; many are shaped like drumsticks.

ABOVE Cantabrian heath (*Daboecia cantabrica* 'Atropurpurea') provides excellent ground cover and colour.

ABOVE Campion (*Silene armeria* 'Electra') is a free-flowering deep pink that gives a late summer show.

ABOVE 'Jer'Rey' is an excellent two-tone pelargonium that creates a strong display on its own.

ABOVE *Pelargonium* 'Rollisson's Unique' can grow 45cm (18in) high, and looks best highlighted in a pot.

ABOVE *Lampranthus* need dry conditions and are perfect for rock crevices or well-drained rockeries.

# hot pink

**The sharper kinds of pink** are nearly on a par with purple, and can be used in big bold shows by growing large shrubs and climbers. In fact using this rich, zingy colour gives you a chance to include some high performance plants from spring to autumn.

Start off the show with a rhododendron like the award-winning 'Rose Bud', which has rose-pink flowers in spring, and follow it with a range of summer roses. 'Zéphirine Drouhin', 3.6m (12ft) high, has the three virtues of being highly scented, thornless and happy on north walls, while the slightly shorter 'Pink Perpétué' is good climbing up a pillar. The geraniums give a huge range of pinks in the border, with *Geranium* x *riversleaianum* 'Russell Pritchard' being one of the strongest. In the autumn, aim for swathes of *Colchicum speciosum* under deciduous trees, which stand out all the more because the flowers open before the leaves begin to appear. Make sure that all the strong pinks get a chance to stand out by keeping them well away from any sharper colours.

TOP Pinks (*Dianthus*) work well with shamrock (*Oxalis*) in this old copper bucket.

ABOVE High impact displays of gladioli need a sheltered sunny spot with good drainage.

deep beds filled with **glossy** pink **perennials**

RIGHT Azaleas love acid soil and make a startling show in late spring.

# Mexican painted pots

Garden containers can sometimes be dull and it is fun to brighten them up to create a splash of colour on your patio or windowbox. The inspiration here was Mexican motifs but you can be inventive and try different designs. Complete the effect by planting up the pots with vibrant pelargoniums in brilliant reds and pinks.

1 Mark the stripes on the pot using masking tape. Vary the widths of the tape to get variation in the finished design. Bear in mind that the areas covered will remain natural terracotta.

3 Paint the coloured stripes, changing colour after each band of masking tape. Allow to dry completely. Peel off the masking tape to reveal coloured stripes alternating with the terracotta.

2 Completely paint the main body of the pot with undercoat, painting over the masking tape as well. Allow to dry according to the manufacturer's instructions.

4 Using the fine artist's brush and the undercoat, paint simple motifs over the stripes. When completely dry, coat the painted area with varnish.

# pale pink

Pale pinks and peachy colours are on offer at all heights, from down by your ankle to climbers high in the trees. Being soft and quiet they are unobtrusive and yet demand a closer look, so it is well worth giving them extra space where you can appreciate their form and texture. The fuchsias in particular always attract plenty of praise.

ABOVE There are dozens of exquisite pink camellias; many are quite tender and need a conservatory.

ABOVE Tulips come in all shapes and sizes; don't overlook little beauties like this.

ABOVE Stone cress (*Aethionema grandiflorum*) is a 25cm (10in) high perennial for a late spring show.

ABOVE *Camellia* 'Lady Loch' is a genuine beauty making a rounded shape covered with pale pink flowers.

ABOVE If you like the large-flowering *Clematis* 'Nelly Moser', try 'Bees Jubilee' because it's even brighter.

ABOVE *Rhododendron* 'Pink Pearl' makes a big, open shape, and is a real eye catcher in the spring.

ABOVE Autumn crocuses (*Colchicum*) provide a cheerful splash of colour when many plants are past flowering.

ABOVE *Rosa* 'Albertine' is a prolific rambler with salmon-pink flowers that readily grows 6m (20ft) high.

ABOVE Tender rose bay (*Nerium oleander*) flowers in summer. It is a good choice for conservatories.

ABOVE Like most pot plants, begonias can be stood outside over summer to inject colour into any gaps.

ABOVE Not all poppies (*Papaver*) have gutsy, blood-red flowers; many are gentle pastels.

ABOVE Fuchsias such as 'Silver Dawn' add a different scale to the garden with their soft-coloured flowers.

ABOVE Stonecrop (*Sedum*) is a big-value, fail-safe summer and autumn plant, providing a big show of flowers.

ABOVE *Verbena* 'Peaches and Cream' is an increasingly popular annual with spreading branching growth.

ABOVE *Rosa* 'Breath of Life' is a scented mini-climber that will not grow much higher than 2.4m (8ft).

ABOVE *Fuchsia* 'Monterey' has a strong vivid colour, and flowers that resemble hovering insects.

# gentle pink

**Soft, gentle pink is a highly** underrated colour. If your garden suffers from any harsh outrageous features, trail soft pink climbers all over them, or group pots of pink fuchsias around them, and completely upgrade the scene. It is also well worth growing one or two really exquisite special pinks in pots for standing on a terrace or eating area, where they will catch the eye and act as a kind of instant, elaborate flower arrangement. The key point with shapely pinks, though, is not to lose them against a massed background in the border. Give them room to show off. And place the autumn-flowering pinks where the sun's more orange rays will catch them, giving them extra warmth and glow.

## inspiring
### shades of **fresh** pink

RIGHT 'Cotton Candy' is one of the very best fuchsias. It is free-flowering, of medium height and has a sprightly, upright shape. Regular 'pinching out' encourages even more flowers.

FAR RIGHT TOP *Rosa* 'Ispahan' is a choice, old-fashioned Damask rose that has scented pink flowers. It is one of the best of its kind because it has a long flowering period.

FAR RIGHT BOTTOM Hebes can make big shrubs, but there are many small ones that are ideal for pots. Painting the container helps bring out the colour of the flowers.

# blue

Woodland bluebells (*Hyacinthoides*) are a terrific sight, not because they're growing in any way 'naturally' and free, but because of three key factors. First, the colour stands out that much more in light shade, second, it is highlighted by a light green grassy background and third, the bluebells spread in large numbers and take the eye further and further away. While it's hard to repeat the last point in the garden, you can aim to give the blues some slight degree of shade to make them stand out even more brightly and vividly. When arranging blues, note that other plants can be used to nudge them into the foreground, just as blues can be used to highlight whites. One of the very best royal blues for the garden is *Anchusa azurea* 'Loddon Royalist'. It has got to be top of your list.

*Iris* 'Dusky Challenger'

# purple-blue

There is no excuse for not having plenty of rich dark blues and purples in the garden. You can use it as a special feature, letting the annual morning glory (*Ipomoea*) scramble up a wigwam of canes, spreading as a carpet on the ground with Dalmatian bellflower (*Campanula portenschlagiana*), or in bushes of scented French lavender (*Lavandula stoechas*).

ABOVE One of the most gorgeous ipomoeas, Morning glory (*Ipomoea indica*) is easily grown from seed.

ABOVE *Lavandula pinnata*, originally from the Canary Islands, is a late summer-flowering shrub.

ABOVE *Vinca minor* 'Aureovariegata' gives first-rate ground cover and masses of blue flowers all summer.

ABOVE French lavender (*Lavandula stoechas*) is small and bushy with masses of dark purple flowers.

ABOVE There is a great range of blue geraniums that thrive just about anywhere, giving colour all summer.

ABOVE The violet flowers of the annual *Nicandra physalodes* are followed by masses of berries.

ABOVE The blue bellflower *Campanula carpatica* produces open, disc-like flowers all summer.

ABOVE *Anemone blanda* is one of the best slightly purple perennials for livening up the spring garden.

ABOVE *Triteleia laxa* gives a good show in early summer, but it needs a sunny position and hates frost.

ABOVE Crocuses can provide colour for nine months of the year; *Crocus nudiflorus* is the one for autumn.

ABOVE Dalmatian bellflower (*Campanula portenschlagiana*) is a robust evergreen about ankle high.

ABOVE The clear, soft blue flowers of *Iris pallida* subsp. *pallida* emerge from beautiful silvery bracts in spring.

ABOVE Jerusalem sage (*Pulmonaria saccharata*) gives two-tone spring colour and has attractive leaves.

ABOVE The mourning widow (*Geranium phaeum*) has such deep purple flowers that they look black.

ABOVE The flowers of *Rhododendron* 'Penheale Blue' are slightly violet-blue when they open in early spring.

ABOVE The blue flag iris (*Iris versicolor*) makes tall flowering clumps round the edge of a pond.

205

# indigo blue

**You need to have several great blues** in the garden in each season to set off the rest of the planting. The good news is that there are plenty of first-rate plants. In spring the California lilac (*Ceanothus* 'Blue Mound') erupts in a great 1.5m (5ft) high mound, though if you fancy a bigger show *Ceanothus arboreus* 'Trewithen Blue' can cover 6 x 8m (20 x 25ft). In summer you can let clematis romp up pillars and posts, and use the likes of buddleja to provide an aerial mass of blue flowers that attract thousands of butterflies. *Salvia uliginosa* starts performing in late summer with long thin open stems topped by bright pale blue flowers. Contrast any darker blues with whites and yellows to highlight their rich tones.

ABOVE When you think the garden is full up, start adding vertical structures and you can send up a huge range of colourful climbers, such as this flamboyant clematis.

LEFT Grape hyacinths (*Muscari latifolium*) offer a wonderful, rich deep blue and look good in clumps in borders or patio pots.

RIGHT These vivid convolvulus are set off beautifully by the blue rim of the pot.

**You Will Need**

1 medium to large
blue pot
Selection of old crocks
or large stones
Soil-based compost
(soil mix)
10 pretty pink,
midseason tulips, such
as *Tulipa* 'Ester'
4 *Viola* x *wittrockiana*
(pansy), such as two-
toned 'Marina', 'Violet
with Blotch', 'Light Blue'
or 'True Blue'

# springtime blues

Blues, mauves and pinks are pretty, fresh colours that are easy on the eye in spring. This sky-blue container sets off the soft mauves and pinks of the pansies and tulips beautifully; similar containers can be found at most garden centres. The same effect can also be created when planting up a windowbox.

1 Cover the base of the pot with a 5cm (2in) layer of drainage material, such as old crocks. Half-fill the pot with a soil-based compost (soil mix) containing lots of grit, vital for drainage.

3 Plant the ten tulip bulbs in two circles, spacing them out evenly and making sure they are not touching each other or the sides of the pot, so they have plenty of room for growth.

2 If you prefer, as an alternative, use a peat-based compost (soil mix) with a layer of grit mixed thoroughly in the bottom half, again to ensure good drainage in winter.

4 Bring the compost level to within 2.5cm (1in) of the top of the pot. Plant the four winter-flowering pansies. The result is a glorious spring display of soft pinks and blues.

# mauve-blue

The blues and purples might be the plants that catch the eye, and they're clearly rich, powerful colours, but too many together can end up being slightly gloomy. Include some paler, lighter mauves because these are extremely good for brightening things up. They do need to be grouped with great care, however, as their effect can be lost against a pale or whitish background. Place plants with beautiful, interesting shapes, such as the North American *Camassia cusickii*, in front of darker backgrounds that will really show them up.

ABOVE *Clematis* 'Mrs Cholmondeley' flourishes in early summer with a mass of light mauve flowers.

ABOVE *Convolvulus sabatius* needs a fast-draining sunny position to flower all summer.

ABOVE The pale blue, scented chimney bellflower (*Campanula pyramidalis*) loves dry, sunny parts of the garden.

ABOVE *Aster* x *frikartii* 'Monch' makes a superb clump of light blue flowers in late summer and early autumn.

ABOVE The Spanish/North African *Geranium malviflorum* with wide, red-veined, pale blue flowers.

ABOVE This alpine *Campanula* will spread to create a blue carpet of tiny, blue, star-like flowers.

ABOVE *Corydalis flexuosa* thrives in shady, rich, well-drained soil, and can also be planted in rockeries.

ABOVE For ground cover with a difference, try *Pratia pedunculata* which thrives even in hot, dry weather.

ABOVE Sweet William (*Phlox divaricata*) flowers in early summer in a wide range of colours, including pale blue.

ABOVE The clump-forming *Scilla peruviana* has a lovely spread of star-shaped flowers in early summer.

ABOVE Prostrate speedwell (*Veronica prostrata*) quickly spreads, making a low carpet of early summer flowers.

ABOVE Baby blue eyes (*Nemophila menziesii*) is an American annual with bright blue flowers.

ABOVE One of the key plants in any blue border is the highly popular *Sisyrinchium* 'California Skies'.

ABOVE The Spanish bluebell (*Hyacinthoides hispanica*) makes a terrific show in a damp, shady spot.

ABOVE *Camassia cusickii* peps things up in late spring with pale blue flowers on top of 75cm (30in) spikes.

# calming mauve

**Mauve is cool and chic**. It is the best colour for giving parts of the garden a clear-cut, elegant theme. Formal, stylized lawns with statues and urns, window boxes against whitewashed houses, and minimalist gardens where shape counts much more than the planting, are all prime contenders for the wide range of mauves available. Mix them with soft pastels such as pinks, greys and cream for the best results.

You can also use mauve in blocks at repeat intervals to act as dividers along a border with much brasher colours, and to highlight and be highlighted by neighbouring stronger tones in a mixed scheme.

## restful and
## soothing waves of mauve

RIGHT The architectural style of the garden is emphasized by the use of an urn on a pedestal, and a knot garden with interweaving patterns. The surrounding colour scheme is unashamedly gorgeous, using a mass of lavender (*Lavandula*).

FAR RIGHT TOP Frame statues that could otherwise be lost to view with thin, elegant spires of colour, using soft pastels that will enhance and not compete with the figure.

FAR RIGHT BOTTOM Flowering window boxes are an excellent way of softening a white exterior. You only need a few attractive plants that flower through the summer to achieve this simple, stylish effect.

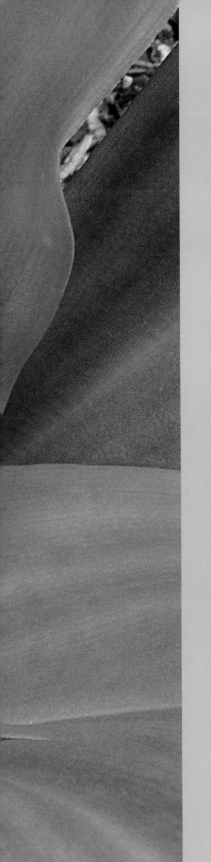

# green

You might not see green as a colour for high summer when the rest of the garden is in top gear, but in spring, after months of mud and splatter, the massive eruption of fresh green foliage makes it the most invigorating sight of the year. This is when green is the star colour, but thereafter it becomes a backdrop, setting off everything else. Not that it has to be. If you choose striking, shapely plants, they'll get as much attention as anything else will. *Gunnera manicata* has strong vertical stems and rough crinkly leaves, like flattened satellite dishes just above your head. You'll also need plenty of evergreens, such as Mexican orange blossom (*Choisya ternata*), to keep the garden alive out of season; the shinier the leaves the better to make the most of the winter sun.

*Eucomis bicolor*

# dark green

Dark green is an exceptional background colour to make white or pale flowers really stand out, and for that you need at least one preferably evergreen shrub or bamboo. The contrast can be just as effective using smart variegated foliage where the leaves have strong white or cream markings. And where you get rich green leaves topped by white, the effect is even better.

ABOVE Grow sages in herb gardens and in any good border, using them to link all kinds of colour schemes.

ABOVE Yew (*Taxus baccata*), makes great topiary and an excellent dark background for white flowers.

ABOVE 'June' is a terrific new hosta that mixes rich blue-green colouring with yellow around the middle.

ABOVE Greek oregano (above) and marjoram are closely related, but the former has the stronger scent.

ABOVE *Hedera helix* 'Congesta' is a non-climbing ivy that makes a small, neat bush about 45cm (18in) high.

ABOVE Common tansy (*Tanacetum vulgare*) has shapely, elegant leaves and bright yellow summer flowers.

ABOVE *Pseudosasa japonica* is a first-rate bamboo that makes a tall thicket with shiny dark green leaves.

ABOVE The Japanese painted fern (*Athyrium niponicum* var. 'Pictum') has wonderful bluish-green leaves.

ABOVE *Hosta ventricosa* 'Variegata' has spinach green leaves with a cream margin.

ABOVE *Sasa palmata* is a Japanese bamboo that normally reaches 6m (20ft), but twice that in dense shade.

ABOVE *Hosta undulata* becomes known as *H. u.* var. *univittata* when the central white stripe appears.

ABOVE The bamboo *Pleioblastus simonii* 'Variegatus' has striped, pointy leaves up to 20cm (8in) long.

ABOVE *Shibataea kumasasa* is a slender-stemmed bamboo, which forms mounds of dark green foliage.

ABOVE Aleutian maidenhair fern (*Adiantum aleuticum*) perks up any semi-shady area with its fine fronds.

ABOVE *Sasa veitchii* is a moderate 1.5m (5ft) high bamboo that romps through woods in the wild.

ABOVE *Levisticum officinale* is a shapely, strong-growing perennial with yellowish flowers in midsummer.

# forest green

**Rich, lively, jungle greens** are a brilliant way of creating an instant atmosphere. You can either go the whole way – using layers and layers of plants, building them up from the ground, ending up with climbers and trees – or you can be much more subtle. A few ferns in any shady spot gives immediate extra interest, while topiary balls, pyramids, spirals and cones add year-round style and impact. You can use the latter as extra, moveable features, or to enliven any flight of steps. You could even create one long, flowing shape, like a sinuous, baroque kind of octopus, by growing it in several sections, each plant in its own container.

## deep beds filled with **luscious, verdant** foliage

ABOVE LEFT A good mix of ferns and hostas (in the bottom right-hand corner). Hostas are invariably grown for their marvellous leaves, many of which have excellent white markings.

LEFT Topiary box (*Buxus*) plants are readily available in most garden centres. Alternatively, you can clip the plants into shape yourself.

RIGHT Any garden can be given a Victorian makeover with a few simple ingredients such as a statue and ferns.

# green mosaic table

## You Will Need

Tracing paper and
pencil
Marine plywood or
exterior grade plywood,
13mm (1/2 in) thick
PVA (white) glue
Paintbrush
Glass mosaic tiles in
off-white, light verdigris,
dark verdigris, moss,
gold-veined verdigris,
gold-veined green
Tile nippers
Goggles
Flexible knife
Cement-based, water-
resistant tile adhesive
Cement-based, water-
resistant grout
Small bucket
Grout spreader
Sponge and soft cloth
Rubber gloves

The soft greens and golds used in the simple flower design of this mosaic table make for a striking piece of furniture, which looks great with lush foliage. It can be used outdoors in good weather, but you will need to bring it inside during very rainy periods and for the winter because it is not completely weatherproof.

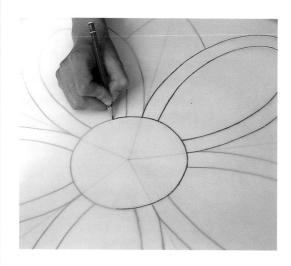

1 Mark out the design for the tabletop, then transfer it to a large sheet of tracing paper. Turn the tracing paper upside down on to the plywood and rub the pattern through to the wood.

3 Mix up the tile adhesive and spread a thin layer over one area at a time. Select the tiles you want and press them into the tile adhesive, leaving a tiny gap between each piece.

2 Seal the marked out plywood with the PVA (white) glue, then cut the tiles into small pieces using tile nippers. Make a pile of each colour and save some to chip into different sizes later on.

4 Scatter the gold-veined tiles among the plain ones to create a subtle sheen. To achieve a neat finish around corners, clip the tiles into wedge shapes with the tile nippers.

# an **elegant** table
## perfect for a lush
# **garden**

5 Continue to fill in the whole design, using the tile nippers to trim the tiles so they fit snugly into the pattern. Once it is complete, leave the tabletop to dry for at least a day.

6 Mix the grout and push it into all the cracks. Wipe over with a damp sponge and polish with a dry cloth. Once dry, turn the tabletop over and spread the base with adhesive to seal it.

# pale green

Every good garden should have a selection of evergreens with differently shaped leaves to link up the summer plants, and to keep the garden alive in winter. It is essential that you make sure that one green tone does not dominate though. Adding lime greens, pale greens, olive greens, cabbage greens etc, will give a much wider, more relaxed range of hues.

ABOVE *Hosta* 'Birchwood Parky's Gold' has yellow-green leaves that give a lift to shady parts of the garden.

ABOVE Ivy (*Hedera helix* 'Golden Ingot') creates a fresh summery look, and is good on long, low walls.

ABOVE The lovely lime-coloured, white-edged leaves of *Hosta* 'Shade Fanfare' turn even paler with age.

ABOVE There are hundreds of different ivies (*Hedera*) in all shades, and the lighter ones make a good backdrop.

ABOVE Architectural plants such as grasses come in a wide range of pale green shades.

ABOVE Lime-green euphorbia is invaluable, providing highlights and contrast in a strong colour scheme.

ABOVE Grasses are back in fashion, such as this *Carex hachijoensis*, which makes a small, lush mound.

ABOVE *Arundo donax* is not in fact a bamboo, but a perennial grass that can grow to 5m (15ft) high.

ABOVE *Pelargonium* 'Mr Henry Cox' is one of the best of its kind if you want patterned leaves with green.

ABOVE Japanese rush (*Acorus gramineus*), an aquatic perennial, adds glossy green colour to ponds.

ABOVE *Gunnera manicata* is ideal if you have a big, damp, boggy space where it can open its massive leaves.

ABOVE *Helichrysum petiolare* is a low, spreading evergreen with white flowers at the end of summer.

ABOVE Italian buckthorn (*Rhamnus alaternus* 'Argenteovariegata') has good foliage, flowers and red fruit.

ABOVE *Pennisetum orientale* is a small grass with beautiful spikelets tinged with a faint purple colour.

ABOVE Silvery-leaved lamb's ears (*Stachys byzantina*) mixes well with this blue-flowering *Nepeta*.

ABOVE The eye-catching *Eryngium giganteum* has spiky green foliage and pale, silvery blue flowers.

223

# mellow green

**When you can't decide** what colour goes right next to a dark or blue-leaved plant, take the colour scheme down a notch by adding a superb pale green. From the blue-tinged kind to ones with a yellowish hue, they add a sense of quiet and space, a pause in the mood of the garden. Conifers, from tiny, hard compact mounds to tall evergreen, vertical chopsticks, are very useful and come in every shade of green, some even verging on black. They also add a sharp sculptural feel. Euphorbias are even livelier, many having smart shapes and pale green involucres like tiny saucers at the tops of the stems. Soft, mellow green is incredibly versatile. Grow it, link it, try it.

FAR LEFT **A sensational display of grasses offer soothing colours as well as architectural interest.**

ABOVE LEFT **A grouping of conifers in the fore-ground, with variegated hostas behind.**

ABOVE RIGHT **A shady, quiet corner is livened up by an attractive fern.**

# white

White might not seem like a colour, but it is; it is actually made up of all the other colours combined, and that's why white goes with anything. You could even try to make a white garden, but if you aim for exclusively white you'll find the glare of midsummer can make it unremittingly forceful and hard. It would be far better to make the garden largely white, injecting plenty of other colours to add rich contrasts during the day. The white stands out in a near magical way at dusk, though, as if the flowers were tiny light bulbs. This effect is most thrilling when a white climbing rose, hanging from a tree, is lit by a full moon. And because white is such a dominant, forceful colour it is best to check that the plants are shapely and worth a much closer look. White is one colour that really does capture the eye.

*Allium sativum*

# white

Whites don't have to be in solid blocks to make a great feature, extraordinarily beautiful though flowers such as lilies and roses are. Whites can create tall, thin verticals, with foxgloves (*Digitalis*), and in the case of *Crambe cordifolia* a fantastic aerial speckling of hundreds of tiny white flowers during the first half of summer.

ABOVE *Rosa* 'Climbing Iceberg' easily grows 3m (10ft) high, and produces lashings of flowers all summer.

ABOVE *Rosa* 'Pascali' is white with a dash of cream, and provides a fine supply of highly attractive flowers.

ABOVE This 1.5m (5ft) high *Dahlia* 'Porcelain' with a hint of lilac is best grown at the back of the border.

ABOVE The rock garden is the best place for this low-growing early summer *Saxifraga paniculata*.

ABOVE Common white foxgloves (*Digitalis purpurea*) really stand out among brighter colours.

ABOVE *Galtonia candicans* is a big-value, tall South African perennial that flowers at the end of summer.

ABOVE Patches of *Allium nigrum*, often with a lilac tinge, make a terrific sight in the early summer border.

ABOVE Cantabrian heath (*Daboecia cantabrica* 'Snowdrift') continues to flower all summer long.

ABOVE Foxtail lilies (*Eremurus*) spice things up with late spring spires that can reach 3m (10ft) high.

ABOVE *Arabis caucasica* 'Flore Pleno' is a rare plant that has pure white, scented flowers.

ABOVE *Crambe cordifolia* has criss-cross stems, creating an aerial balloon, with scores of tiny flowers.

ABOVE *Rhododendron decorum* stages a spectacular late spring to early summer show with scented flowers.

ABOVE *Achillea ageratifolia* produces a mass of flowers that make a fine low link at the front of the border.

ABOVE *Camellia* 'Cornish Snow' grows into a big shrub, packed with flowers that are tinged pink on opening.

ABOVE *Osteospermum caulescens* keeps low and spreads wide, creating a mat of daisy-like flowers.

ABOVE There are many lilies in white and cream, the more intriguing ones with a speckling along the petals.

# clean whites

**If you think spring has to mean yellow**, that is daffodils, daffodils and more daffodils, you're mistaken. There are plenty of quite beautiful whites to start off the new year. Stylish tulips take some beating, like 'Spring Green' and the extremely popular 'White Triumphator', which has a beautiful slender flower that stands about 60cm (2ft) high. White tulips are best highlighted by dwarf box (*Buxus*) hedging or a dark green background such as yew (*Taxus*). Other star white spring plants include anemones, camellias, *Clematis armandii*, magnolias and ornamental cherry (*Prunus*).

LEFT *Rhododendron* 'Loder's White' offers a burst of fresh colour in spring.

ABOVE Lily-of-the-valley (*Convallaria majalis*) makes exquisitely scented ground cover.

RIGHT The taller tulips always look better when they are underplanted with a complementary colour, like these white daisies.

# summery whites

**Gardens need fresh whites** to lift and brighten displays, and provide an instant, highly effective contrast that will emphasize magentas, dark reds and yellows. It gives an all-round spark. You can either stick to individual plants that will hold their own, keep their shape and remain completely distinct, or opt for twisters, scramblers and climbers that don't have to grow vertically, but can happily spiral their way horizontally through and over adjacent plants. Use medium-sized shrubs to give clematis and roses a leg-up, and to provide a horticultural shelf for them to charge over.

# refreshing flashes
## of crisp white

FAR LEFT While the large-flowering roses catch the eye, smaller, delicate, more elegant ones are at times just what you need to create the perfect display.

LEFT Plant *Solanum jasminoides* 'Album' next to an evergreen, such as a holly, and let it scramble its way up, making a great showy mass of white flowers all summer.

BELOW The white flowers of these tobacco plants (*Nicotiana*) and heliotrope (*Heliotropium*) leap out with even more gusto than normal because of the contrasting terracotta colouring and the abundant rich green leaves.

# colour
## combinations

The key to a look like this (left) is to make sure you grow plants in lively, contrasting blocks of colour. Tulips give the most astonishing spring displays, and they can be as jazzy or as cool as you like. You can underplant the whole scheme with forget-me-nots (*Myosotis sylvatica*), which provide a blue backing. If you want to see how you can upgrade the scheme, ignore all talk about taste and fashion and see what artists like Jackson Pollock and van Gogh did with a paintbrush. Be brave, mix colours and make sure you grab the eye. Whether you choose the classic combinations of blue and white, or red and yellow, or more exciting mixtures of purple and orange, or lime green and turquoise, the possibilities are endless.

# classics

**Some colour combinations are always good**, no matter where they are grown. Yellow and blue, red and white, blue and pink, paired up these always look sensational. The trick is to spot which colours and which plants work well in major gardens, and then to copy the idea in your own garden. Huge houses with acres of land might be able to provide a better backdrop and more elaborate scale, but all gardening means reinventing, rescaling and adapting ideas to suit your needs. And if the combinations do work, put them right at the front where they will "carry" any neighbouring plants and give them a special lift.

## snappy, **primary** shades create **stunning** borders

ABOVE Two rows, two colours, and the result is totally stylish.

LEFT A wide mix of traditional blooms gives an easy flow.

RIGHT A smart group of 'Striped Belladonna' tulips.

# pastels

**Every garden needs quiet,** exquisite moments using soft pinks, white and mauve. Such schemes work infinitely better if they are given plenty of space where they can create their own special mood; they should not be crammed into a spare hidden corner. The scheme will be even more sumptuous if you can include plenty of plants that have rich scents; mock orange blossom (*Philadelphus*) and old shrub roses such as *Rosa* 'Charles de Mills' are essential.

# soothing and
# calming blues and creams

FAR LEFT An enterprising mix
of love-in-a-mist (*Nigella
damascena*), with a sensational
cream-coloured climbing rose.

LEFT Flatter an interesting statue
with pastel roses, clematis and
foxgloves (*Digitalis*).

BELOW A two-tone classic
summer combination using a
swirl of pale cream roses set
off by blue phlox.

239

ABOVE Flash-red Dahlia 'Bishop of Llandaff' backed by blue asters.

LEFT Purple alliums and orange *Eremurus* provide complementary shapes.

RIGHT A stunning display of Himalayan blue poppies (*Meconopsis*), lime-green euphorbia and orange 'Warm Welcome' climbing roses.

# contemporary

**The colourful garden of the 21st century needs shape, style** and a "look-at-me-now" air. Use bright, strong colours in challenging, unexpected ways. Architectural plants with zany stems and blobs of colour on top need their own space where their look can unfold. Also, go for strong contrasts using just two colours; don't let visitors rest in a stupefying soft soup of pastels designed to send them to sleep. Keep their eyes alert, bring primary colours up close and then use these colours far away. Best of all, work with and then break their assumptions about colour. Use colour in the garden as if it were brand new.

# seasonal gardening tips

## SPRING

### What to Plant

- Container-grown trees and shrubs
- Gladioli and summer bulbs
- Hanging baskets
- Hedges
- Herbaceous plants and also stake them
- Sweet peas sown last autumn
- Finish planting bare-rooted trees and shrubs
- Divide dahlia tubers that are sprouting
- Divide and replant congested vigorous perennials

BELOW Furniture and other accessories can be used to inject colour into a garden as well as plants.

### What to Prune

- Dogwoods (*Cornus*), thinning them out
- *Eucalyptus gunnii*, for new coloured stems
- Evergreen shrubs that need clipping
- Overgrown deciduous hedges
- Roses, if they have not already been done
- Shrubs that flower on new growth (e.g. buddlejas)
- Winter-flowering heathers
- Pinch out the tips of fuchsias to make them bush out, or train them as standards

### What to Sow

- Hardy annuals
- Harden off tender bedding plants

### What to Feed

- Add slow-release fertilizer to the compost of container plants
- Beds and borders while wet after heavy rain

### Lawns and Ponds

- Make a new lawn from seed or turf, and repair worn patches
- Mow established lawns regularly from now on starting with a high cut
- Plant and stock new ponds with oxygenators

### Extras

- Beware of late frosts and protect tender growth
- Spring clean and ventilate the greenhouse
- Deadhead the flowers of bulbs, and let the foliage die down naturally

• Tidy up the rock garden, and apply fresh stone chippings where necessary

## SUMMER

### In the Flower Garden

• Finish hardening off and planting out tender bedding plants

• Dead-head plants in borders and containers regularly

• Plant dahlias and later give a tomato feed, and water regularly

• Hoe beds and borders to eliminate weeds

• Lift and store tulip bulbs

• Mow lawns planted with spring bulbs

• Plant autumn-flowering bulbs (e.g. colchicums)

• Plant out summer bedding

• Buy new plants

• Tie in new shoots on climbers

• Thin hardy annuals

• Watch for signs of mildew and aphids on roses, and spray promptly if found

• Apply a rose fertilizer once the main flush of flowering is over

### What to Propagate

• Layer border carnations

• Start sowing hardy annuals to overwinter

• Take semi-ripe cuttings of fuchsias and pelargoniums, etc.; early and midsummer are the best times to propagate

### What to Sow

• Biennials such as wallflowers and forget-me-nots

• Fast-growing annuals such as sunflowers

ABPVE **This rich mixture of yellows, reds and blues has created a stunning summer patio border.**

### What to Prune

• Clip beech, holly, hornbeam and yew hedges

• Cut back and feed delphiniums and lupins after flowering to get a second batch of flowers

• Pinch out the growing tip from early-flowering chrysanthemums

• Broom, lilac, philadelphus, spiraea, wisteria, etc., and exhausted rambler roses after flowering

### Lawns and Ponds

• Remove excessive growth of algae in ponds, leaving some for young frogs to hide in

• Make sure frogs and newts can easily get out of ponds, and add nearby hiding places

• Mow the lawn, except in very dry weather, and never scalp it

• Top up water levels in ponds. Only add fish if you haven't got frogs, or they'll eat the young

## Extras

• Go on nightly patrols armed with a torch and bucket, and remove/destroy slugs and snails

• Order bulb catalogues and spring-flowering bulbs for autumn delivery

• Ventilate greenhouses every day, more so when hot, and water regularly

BELOW *Tulipa kolpakowskiana.*

# AUTUMN

## In the Flower Garden

• Collect ripe seed; store in airtight containers

• Cut down and lift dahlias blackened by frost; store for next year

• Cut down the dead tops of herbaceous perennials

• Lift and store gladioli and other tender bulbs, corms and tubers

• Lift and take in chrysanthemums not hardy enough to overwinter outside

## What to Plant

• Bare-rooted shrubs and winter trees (including roses) from now to late winter

• Lilies and spring-flowering bulbs such as tulips

• Winter window boxes

• Climbers

## What to Sow

• Garlic cloves

• Spring-flowering biennials

• Sweet peas for planting out next spring

## Lawns and Ponds

• Clear fallen leaves and debris out of ponds

• Rake lawns

• Sow new lawns

## Extras

• Clean out and insulate greenhouses

• Clear summer bedding and prepare for spring bedding plants

• Collect and compost fallen leaves

ABOVE Rich pink flowers in contrasting tones, such as these azaleas, add a splash of colour to any border.

# WINTER

## What to Plant

- Continue planting bare-rooted shrubs and trees
- Divide clumps of snowdrops while still in leaf

## What to Prune

- Wisteria
- Roses in late winter
- Cut back grasses

## Extras

- Build compost heaps
- Check bulbs that have been stored

- Protect slightly tender plants such as some penstemons in cold spells
- Check spring catalogues have been ordered
- Make sure the greenhouse is ventilated even during cold weather if paraffin heaters are used
- Ensure there is enough winter colour in the garden, and plan for next year if there isn't
- If you want to, change the garden's design, or embellish with extra features such as ornamental paths, ponds (but do not line until next spring), pergolas, etc.

# planting guide

This is a checklist of plants that, together with those in the portrait galleries, provide key blocks or flashes of colour. Plants that require ericaceous or acid soil are indicated by an asterisk.

## SPRING

### Yellow

*Adonis amurensis*

Cowslip, primrose (*Primula*)

*Crocus*

Crown imperial (*Fritillaria*)

Daffodil (*Narcissus*)

*Forsythia*

ABOVE *Rosa* 'Just Joey'.

Peony (*Paeonia*)

Primrose (*Primula*)

*Rhododendron* (including azalea)*

Skunk cabbage (*Lysichiton americanus*)

Tulip (*Tulipa*)

Wallflower (*Erysimum*)

### Orange

Crown imperial (*Fritillaria*)

Daffodil (*Narcissus*)

*Physalis*

*Rhododendron* (including azalea)*

Tulip (*Tulipa*)

Wallflower (*Erysimum*)

### Red

*Anemone*

*Bellis perennis*

*Chaenomeles*

Lenten rose (*Helleborus orientalis*)

Peony (*Paeonia*)

Tulip (*Tulipa*)

### Pink

*Bergenia* x *schmidtii*

*Camellia sasanqua*

Crab apple (*Malus*)

*Cyclamen coum*

*Daphne*

Hellebore (*Helleborus orientalis*)

*Nectaroscordum siculum* subsp. *bulgaricum*

Ornamental cherry (*Prunus*) – blossom

Peony (*Paeonia*)

*Pulmonaria*

*Rhododendron* (including azalea)*

Tulip (*Tulipa*)

### Blue

*Anemone blanda*

Bluebell (*Hyacinthoides*)

California lilac (*Ceanothus*)

*Clematis alpina* 'Frances Rivis'

*Crocus*

Forget-me-not (*Myosotis sylvatica*)

Granny's bonnet (*Aquilegia*)

Grape hyacinth (*Muscari*)

Hyacinth (*Hyacinthus*)

*Iris reticulata*

*Pulmonaria*

Rosemary (*Rosmarinus*)

*Scilla siberica*

### White

*Anemone*

*Camellia*

*Chaenomeles*

*Clematis armandii*

Crab apple (*Malus*)

*Crocus*

Daffodil (*Narcissus*)

Dog's tooth violet (*Erythronium*)

*Exochorda* x *macrantha* 'The Bride'

Foam flower (*Tiarella wherryi*)

Honeysuckle (*Lonicera fragrantissima*)

Hyacinth (*Hyacinthus*)

Japanese snowball bush (*Viburnum plicatum*)

*Leucojum* (Snowflake)

Lily-of-the-valley (*Convallaria majalis*)

*Magnolia*

Mexican orange blossom (*Choisya ternata*)

Ornamental cherry (*Prunus*) – blossom

Peony (*Paeonia*)

*Pulmonaria officinalis* 'Sissinghurst White'

*Skimmia japonica*

Tulip (*Tulipa*)

### Green

*Arum italicum* 'Pictum'

*Pulmonaria*

Spurge (*Euphorbia*)

## SUMMER

### Yellow

*Achillea*

*Anthemis*

*Bidens ferulifolia*

Black-eyed Susan (*Rudbeckia*)

*Canna*

Clematis

Coreopsis

Corydalis lutea

Dahlia

Daylily (Hemerocallis)

Evening primrose
(Oenothera)

Helenium

Honeysuckle (Lonicera)

Inula hookeri

Iris

Laburnum

Ligularia

Lily (Lilium)

Marguerite
(Argyranthemum)

Mullein (Verbascum)

Poppy (Papaver)

Potentilla

Robinia pseudoacacia
'Frisia'

Rose (Rosa)

Sunflower (Helianthus)

Zinnia

## Orange

Busy Lizzie (Impatiens)

Crocosmia

Dahlia

Daylily (Hemerocallis)

Geum

Helenium

Honeysuckle (Lonicera)

Lily (Lilium)

Marigold (Calendula,
Tagetes)

Nasturtium (Tropaeolum)

Potentilla

Red-hot poker (Kniphofia)

Rose (Rosa)

Spurge (Euphorbia
griffithii 'Fireglow')

Sunflower (Helianthus)

Zinnia

## Red

Bergamot (Monarda)

Canna

Clematis

Cosmos atrosanguineus

Crocosmia

Dahlia

Daylily (Hemerocallis)

Fuchsia

Geranium phaeum

Geum

Hollyhock (Alcea rosea)

Knautia macedonica

Lobelia

Lupin (Lupinus)

Lychnis coronaria

Nasturtium (Tropaeolum)

Pelargonium

Penstemon

Poppy (Papaver)

Potentilla

Red valerian (Centranthus
ruber)

Rose (Rosa)

Salvia

Zinnia

## Pink

Angel's fishing rod
(Dierama pulcherrimum)

Beauty bush (Kolkwitzia
amabilis)

Clematis

Cranesbill (Geranium)

Dahlia

Foxglove (Digitalis)

Lilac (Syringa)

Penstemon

Pink (Dianthus)

Poppy (Papaver)

Rhodochiton
atrosanguineus

Rock rose (Cistus)

Rose (Rosa)

Salvia

Spider flower (Cleome
hassleriana)

Sweet pea (Lathyrus)

## Blue

Agapanthus

Anchusa azurea 'Loddon
Royalist'

Blue flag (Iris versicolor)

Butterfly bush (Buddleja)

Campanula

Cider gum (Eucalyptus
gunnii)

Clematis

Corydalis flexuosa

Cranesbill (Geranium)

Delphinium

Hydrangea

Jacob's ladder
(Polemonium)

Lavender (Lavandula)

Lilac (Syringa)

Love-in-a-mist
(Nigella)

Meconopsis

Ornamental onion
(Allium)

ABOVE *Pelargonium* 'Sunraysia'.

Penstemon

Salvia

Sea holly (Eryngium)

Solanum crispum
'Glasnevin'

Sweet rocket (Hesperis
matronalis)

Verbena bonariensis

Viola

Wisteria

## White

Agapanthus

Artemesia 'Powis Castle'
– silver foliage

Baby's breath
(Gypsophila paniculata)

Bleeding heart (Dicentra
spectabilis alba)

Clematis

Cornus kousa

Crambe cordifolia

ABOVE *Muscari latifolium.*

Delphinium

Foxglove (*Digitalis*)

*Gaura lindheimeri*

*Geranium*

Golden feverfew
   (*Tanacetum*)

*Hydrangea*

*Iris laevigata*

Lavender (*Lavandula*)

*Leucanthemum*

Lilac (*Syringa*)

Lily (*Lilium*)

Loosestrife (*Lysimachia*)

*Lychnis coronaria* 'Alba'

Marguerite
   (*Argyranthemum*)

Mock orange
   (*Philadelphus*)

Ornamental onion
   (*Allium*)

*Osteospermum*

Rose (*Rosa*)

*Solanum jasminoides*
   'Album'

*Stachys byzantina* – silver
   foliage

Sweet rocket (*Hesperis*
   *matronalis*)

Tobacco plant (*Nicotiana*)

*Wisteria*

### Green

*Agave*

*Alchemilla mollis*

*Angelica*

*Astilboides tabularis*

Banana (*Musa*) – foliage

*Brunnera macrophylla*

Buckler fern (*Dryopteris*)

*Canna* – foliage

Chinese rhubarb (*Rheum*
   *palmatum*)

*Darmera peltata*

Dogwood (*Cornus*)

Elder (*Sambucus*)

*Ensete ventricosum* –
   foliage

Feather grass (*Stipa*)

Feather reed grass
   (*Calamagrostis* x
   *acutiflora*)

Fennel (*Foeniculum*
   *vulgare*)

Fig (*Ficus*)

Grape vine (*Vitis*)

*Gunnera manicata*

Hair grass (*Deschampsia*)

*Hosta*

*Humulus lupulus* 'Aureus'

*Melianthus major*

*Miscanthus*

*Pennisetum*

Purple moor grass
   (*Molinia caerulea*)

*Ricinus communis* –
   foliage

*Rodgersia pinnata*

Sedge (*Carex*)

## AUTUMN
### Yellow

*Acer palmatum** – foliage

*Clematis tangutica*

*Cotoneaster* – berries

*Dahlia*

Firethorn (*Pyracantha*)
   – berries

Rowan (*Sorbus*) – berries

Witch hazel (*Hamamelis*)
   – foliage

### Orange

*Acer palmatum** – foliage

*Amelanchier* – foliage

*Berberis* – foliage

*Cercidiphyllum japonicum*
   – foliage

*Cotinus* – foliage

*Dahlia*

Dogwood (*Cornus*)
   – foliage

Grape vine (*Vitis*)
   – foliage

Firethorn (*Pyracantha*)
   – berries

*Fothergilla* – foliage

*Liquidambar* – foliage

*Nyssa sylvatica* – foliage

Ornamental cherry

(*Prunus*) – foliage

*Physalis alkekengi* –
   berries

Red-hot poker (*Kniphofia*)

*Rhus typhina* – foliage

Rowan (*Sorbus*) – berries

Spindle tree (*Euonymus*)
   – foliage

Virginia creeper
   (*Parthenocissus*) –
   foliage

### Red

*Acer palmatum** – foliage

*Cercis canadensis* 'Forest
   Pansy'

*Cotoneaster* – berries

Crab apples (*Malus*) –
   berries

*Dahlia*

Firethorn (*Pyracantha*)
   – berries

*Fuchsia*

Kaffir lily (*Schizostylis*
   *coccinea* 'Major')

Lords and ladies (*Arum*
   *italicum*) – berries

*Penstemon*

Rose (*Rosa*) – hips

Rowan (*Sorbus*) – berries

*Sedum*

### Pink

*Aster*

*Callicarpa bodinieri* var.
   *giraldi* – berries

*Colchicum*

*Cyclamen*
   *hederifolium*

Dahlia

Kaffir lily (*Schizostyllis coccinea* 'Jennifer')

*Nerine bowdenii*

## Blue

*Aster*

*Gentiana**

Monkshood (*Aconitum*)

*Perovskia* 'Blue Spire'

*Salvia*

## White

*Aster*

Christmas box (*Sarcococca humilis*)

*Crocus laevigatus*

*Gaura lindheimeri*

Japanese anemone (*Anemone* x *hybrida*)

Snowdrop (*Galanthus reginae-olgae*)

Strawberry tree (*Arbutus unedo*)

## Green

See Winter Evergreen

# WINTER

## Yellow

*Clematis cirrhosa*

Daffodil (*Narcissus* 'February Gold')

*Iris danfordiae*

Mahonia

*Phyllostachys vivax aureocaulis* – stems

Winter aconite (*Eranthis hyemalis*)

Winter jasmine (*Jasminum nudiflorum*)

Witch hazel (*Hamamelis*)

## Orange

*Phyllostachys bambusoides* 'Allgold' – bamboo stems

## Red

*Bergenia* 'Bressingham Salmon' – foliage

*Crocus tommasinianus* 'Ruby Giant'

Dogwood – stems (*Cornus alba* 'Sibirica')

*Iris foetidissima* (seeds)

Lenten rose (*Helleborus orientalis*)

*Parrotia persica*

*Prunus*

*Tilia platyphyllos* 'Rubra' – new red twigs

## Pink

*Daphne mezereum*

*Viburnum* x *bodnantense*

## Blue

*Iris reticulata*

*Iris unguicularis*

## White

*Betula utilis* var. *jacquemontii* – bark

Christmas rose (*Helleborus niger*)

*Daphne bholua*

*Erica carnea* 'Golden Starlet'*

*Eucalyptus niphophila* – bark

Lenten rose (*Helleborus orientalis*)

*Rubus cockburnianus* – stems

Snowdrop (*Galanthus*)

*Viburnum tinus*

## Green

*Helleborus argutifolius*

Lenten rose (*Helleborus orientalis*)

## Evergreen

Box (*Buxus*)

*Camellia japonica*

Christmas box (*Sarcococca humilis*)

Chusan palm (*Trachycarpus fortunei*)

*Cordyline australis*

*Cotoneaster*

Cypress (*Cupressus*)

*Daphne odora*

*Elaeagnus pungens*

*Eucalyptus*

*Euonymus fortunei*

False cypress (*Chamaecyparis*)

*Fatsia japonica*

*Garrya elliptica*

*Griselinia littoralis*

Heath (*Erica*)*

Heather (*Calluna*)*

*Hebe*

Holly (*Ilex*)

Ivy (*Hedera*)

*Itea ilicifolia*

Juniper (*Juniperus*)

Lavender (*Lavandula*)

Loquat (*Eriobotrya japonica*)

*Magnolia grandiflora*

*Mahonia*

Mexican orange blossom (*Choisya ternata*)

*Osmanthus*

Pine (*Pinus*)

Portugal laurel (*Prunus lusitanica*)

Privet (*Ligustrum*)

Rosemary (*Rosmarinus*)

Silver fir (*Abies*)

*Skimmia*

Spruce (*Picea*)

*Thuja*

Thyme (*Thymus*)

*Viburnum davidii*

Yew (*Taxus*)

BELOW *Dahlia* 'Ellen Huston'.

# decorating suppliers

**UNITED KINGDOM**

**Atlantis Art Materials**
146 Brick Lane
London EC1 6RU

**Corres Mexican Tiles Ltd**
Unit 1A Station Road
Hampton Wick
Kingston
Surrey KT1 4HG
Tel: 020 8943 4142

**Crown Paints**
Crown Decorative
Products Ltd
P.O. Box 37
Crown House
Hollins Road
Darwen
Lancashire BB3 0BG

**Ellis and Farrier**
20 Beak Street
London W1R 3HA
BEADS, SEQUINS

**Europacrafts**
Hawthorn Avenue
Hull
HU3 5JZ
Tel: 01482 223 399

**John Lewis plc**
Oxford Street
London W1A 1EX
(Branches throughout the
country)
FABRICS, FURNISHING
FABRICS, TRIMMINGS,
RIBBONS, BEADS,
CURTAIN TAPES

**Mosaic Workshop**
1a Princeton Street
London WC1R 4AX
Tel: 020 7404 9249

**Nuline**
315 Westbourne Park Road
London W11
GENERAL HARDWARE,
SHEET METAL SUPPLIERS

**Paint Magic**
79 Shepperton Road
Islington
London N1 3DF

**Panduro Hobby**
Westward House
Transport Avenue
Brentford
Middlesex
TW8 9HF

**E. Ploton Ltd**
273 Archway Road
London
N6 5AA
ART AND GILDING
MATERIALS

**Woolfin Textiles & Co**
64 Great Titchfield Street
London W1
RANGE OF NATURAL
FABRICS,
CALICO,
HESSIAN (BURLAP)

**World's End Tiles**
Silverthorne Road
Battersea
London
SW8 3HE
Tel: 020 7720 8358
RANGE OF TILES

**UNITED STATES**

**Art Essentials of New
York Ltd**
3 Cross Street
Suffern
NY 10901
Tel: (800) 283 5323

**The Art Store**
935 Erie Blvd. E.
Syracuse,
NY 13210

**Dick Blick**
P.O. Box 1267
Galesburg
IL 61402
Tel: (309) 343 6181

**Brian's Crafts
Unlimited**
P.O. Box 731046
Ormond Beach
FL 32173-046
Tel: (904) 672 2726

**Britex Fabrics**
146 Geary Street
San Francisco
CA 94108
FABRICS, WIDE
RANGE OF GENERAL
CRAFT MATERIALS
AND EQUIPMENT

**Createx Colors**
14 Airport Park Road
East Granby
CT 06026
Tel: (860) 653 5505

**Eastern Art Glass**

P.O. Box 341

Wyckoff

NJ 07481

**Hofcraft**

P.O. Box 72

Grand Haven

MI 49417

Tel: (800) 828 0359

**Ideal Tile of
Manhattan. Inc**

405 East 51st St

Peekskill

NY 10022

**Peal Paint**

Canal Street

NY 10011

**CANADA**

**Abbey Arts & Crafts**

4118 East Hastings
  Street

Vancouver BC

Tel: 299 5201

**Lewiscraft**

2300 Yonge Street

Toronto

Ontario M4P 1E4

**AUSTRALIA**

**Camden Arts Centre
Pty Ltd**

188-200 Gertrude Street

Fitzroy

3065

**W M Crosbey
(Merchandise) Pty Ltd**

266-274

King Street

Melbourne

3000

**Hobby Co**

402

Gallery Level

197 Pitt Street

Sydney

Tel: (02) 221 0666

**Rodda Pty Ltd**

62 Beach Street

Port Melbourne

Victoria

**Spotlight (60 stores)**

Tel: (freecall) 1800 500021

# index

## Picture Credits

Jonathan Buckley: pages 14, *172 r*, *174 cl cr*, *175 cl br*, *176*, *177 r,*, *178–9*, *180 br*, *181 cl cc*, *202–3*, *218 t*, *219*, *225 l r*, *236 l*, *240 l r*, *241*.